MARY SHELLEY

SERIES PREFACE

Gothic Authors: Critical Revisions is dedicated to publishing innovative introductory guides to writers of the Gothic. The series explores how new critical approaches and perspectives can help us to recontextualize an author's work in a way that is both accessible and informative. The series publishes work that is of interest to students of all levels and teachers of the literary Gothic and cultural history.

SERIES EDITORS

EDITORIAL BOARD

GOTHIC AUTHORS: CRITICAL REVISIONS

Mary Shelley

Angela Wright

UNIVERSITY OF WALES PRESS
2018

www.uwp.co.uk

British Library CIP Data
A catalogue record for this book is available from the British Library

ISBN (hardback) 978-1-78316-846-0
ISBN (paperback) 978-1-78683-173-6
eISBN 978-1-78316-847-7

Typeset by Biblichor Ltd, Edinburgh
Printed by CPI Antony Rowe, Melksham

For Jessica and Antonia Mathison

Contents

Acknowledgements

The idea for a book which more fully appraised the literary career of Mary Wollstonecraft Shelley as an author working within the Gothic literary mode was first suggested to me around 2010. Due to other commitments and my own anxiety that I could not do justice to Mary Shelley, however, it has taken longer to write than first anticipated. My thanks for getting me beyond this creative impasse are due, first and foremost, to Sarah Lewis, my editor at the University of Wales Press, who has shown encouragement, patience and enthusiasm throughout the writing of the book, and secondly to the anonymous reader who has offered excellent and supportive advice. I also wish to thank my colleague Andy Smith, at the University of Sheffield, who first suggested the idea of this book to me. The book also profited from a period of research leave from the University of Sheffield, and I am grateful to my home department, the School of English, for granting this to me.

I derived considerable inspiration from a trip to the New York Public Library to examine some of Mary Wollstonecraft Shelley's manuscripts in the Carl H. Pforzheimer Collection in 2011. I also wish to thank Dr Elizabeth Denlinger, the curator of this wonderful collection, who corresponded with me about my visit, laid out all of the manuscripts that I requested, and corresponded with me afterwards, consistently offering excellent support and advice. Holding the physical materials handled by Mary Shelley offered me considerable inspiration, and I have been able to make use of some of those materials in the course of my study. My thanks are also due to the British Academy for their financial support of my research trip by means of a Small Research Award.

The notion that we write books in isolation without advice or creative input from anyone else is one that Mary Shelley herself would have disputed. The same holds true for my academic work on her in this book; I am truly grateful for the warmth and encouragement of my colleagues at work, particularly Dr Anna Barton, Professor Joe Bray, Dr Madeleine Callaghan, Dr Hamish Mathison and Professor Andy Smith, who have offered advice, encouragement and feedback during this process. I am truly in your debt, dear colleagues. With Madeleine Callaghan, I also organised a conference during the Summer of 2016 to commemorate the Summer of 1816, and the fun, warmth, insight and generosity of our helpful colleagues, our graduate students and our delegates was truly inspirational. Over the years, I have taught the works of Mary Shelley many times at both undergraduate and graduate level. I am constantly delighted by the enthusiasm, insight and research that my students bring to her works. I thank my students for their continuing engagement with Mary Shelley.

I am also grateful to my friends Sarah Brown and Joy Turnbull who, without being asked, offered assistance with childcare as this manuscript approached its deadline. My family too has been a source of continual support to me. From afar, my parents Robert and Mary Wright have offered continual encouragement, as have my siblings Julia, Martin and Malcolm. My husband Hamish has allowed me time and space to complete this project, offering advice along the way. Our two wonderful daughters, Jessica and Antonia Mathison, have provided me with fun and inspiration, reminding me in their demands to laugh, smile and play. Their routines as young girls have insisted that I raise my nose from my books and take them to their various clubs and parties. This has been invaluable to me, more than they will ever know. In thankfulness for their presence in my life, I dedicate this book to Jessica and Antonia, hoping that they too will continue to write their own stories.

Angela Wright, Sheffield, 2016

Mary Shelley: A Chronology

1756 Birth of William Godwin

1759 Birth of Mary Wollstonecraft

1790 Commissioned by Joseph Johnson, Wollstonecraft publishes *A Vindication of the Rights of Men* in response to Edmund Burke's letter *Reflections on the Revolution in France*

1792 Publication of Wollstonecraft's *Vindication of the Rights of Woman*

1793 Publication of Godwin's *Enquiry Concerning Political Justice*

1794 Publication of Godwin's first novel, *Things as They Are, or the Adventures of Caleb Williams*; birth of Fanny [Frances] Imlay, Wollstonecraft's daughter by Gilbert Imlay

1797 Marriage of Mary Wollstonecraft to William Godwin (29 March); birth of Mary Wollstonecraft Godwin (later to become Mary Shelley) (30 August); death of Mary Wollstonecraft from puerperal fever (10 September)

1798 Godwin publishes the controversially received *Memoir of the Author of a Vindication of the Rights of Woman* and edition of Wollstonecraft's *Posthumous Works*, including her unfinished novel *The Wrongs of Woman, or Maria*

1801 Marriage of William Godwin to Mary Jane Clairmont who, with her two children, Charles and Mary Jane (later to rename herself Claire), moves in to live with Godwin, Mary, and Fanny Imlay in Somers Town (near London, 21 December)

1803 Birth of William Godwin Jr, only child of Godwin and Mary Jane Clairmont

1808 Mary Shelley's first poem, 'Mounseer Nongtongpaw', published by M. J. Godwin and Co., her father's company

1812 Mary travels to Dundee to live with the Baxter family until the following June. On a brief return visit home in November, for the first time Mary meets Percy Bysshe Shelley, recently married to Harriet Westbrook; he has become a frequent visitor to her father's home (November)

1814 Mary returns to London; meets Percy Shelley again and a relationship develops between the two, who often conduct their secret meetings in St Pancras Churchyard, where Mary Wollstonecraft is buried (May and June); elopes with Percy to the Continent, with her stepsister Claire Clairmont (28 July); they travel in France, Germany, Switzerland and Holland (July and August); purchase green notebook that is to become their collective journal where they record what they have read and what they have visited; both return to England (September), where Percy Shelley hides from creditors, avoiding arrest for debt

1815 Mary gives birth to her first daughter (22 February), who dies (6 March); move to Bishopsgate, Windsor (August)

1816 Birth of son William (24 January); second trip to the Continent with Percy Shelley and Claire Clairmont (who is pregnant with Byron's child); meeting with Lord Byron and John Polidori in Geneva at the Villa Diodati (May); genesis of *Frankenstein* in the ghost story competition at the Villa Diodati (June); visit to Chamonix (July); return to England (September); suicide of Mary's half-sister Fanny Imlay (9 October); suicide of Percy's wife, Harriet Westbrook, who is found in the Serpentine five days later (10 December); marriage of Mary Wollstonecraft Godwin and Percy Shelley (30 December)

1817 Birth of Claire Clairmont's daughter Alba by Byron (later to be renamed Allegra) (12 January); Percy Shelley loses custody of his two children by Harriet Westbrook; move to Marlow (March); *Frankenstein* completed (14 May); birth of daughter Clara (2 September); publication of *History of a Six Weeks' Tour*, a collaboration with Percy Shelley (T. Hookham and C. and J. Ollier; December)

1818 Publication of *Frankenstein; or, The Modern Prometheus* (Lackington, Hughes, Harding, Mayor and Jones; January); departure for Italy with Shelley, Claire and Alba (March); settle in Bagna di Luca (June); move to Este; death of Clara (September); move to Rome (November); move to Naples (December); Mary undertakes historical reading that will contribute to *Castruccio, Prince of Lucca*, later to be renamed *Valperga*

1819 Move back to Rome (March) where son William Shelley dies (7 June); move to Livorno (June); begins writing *Matilda* (August); move to Florence (September); birth of her only surviving child Percy Florence (12 November)

1820 Move to Pisa (January); completion of *Matilda* (February); composes poetic dramas *Proserpine* and *Midas* (April and May); move back to Livorno (June); move to Bagni di San Giuliano (August); begins writing of *Valperga;* move to Pisa (October)

1821 Return to Bagni di San Giuliano (April); finishes *Valperga* (August–December); move to Pisa (October); sends *Valperga* (still called *Castruccio, Prince of Lucca*) to Godwin for publication, granting him permission to use the proceeds to pay off debt

1822 Death of Allegra Byron, daughter of Claire and Lord Byron (31 March); move to Lerici (May); miscarriage (16 June); death of Percy Shelley while sailing with Edward Williams in the Gulf of Spezia (8 July); Shelley's body cremated at Viareggio (August); moves to Genoa (September)

1823 Publication of *Valperga* (Colburn and Bentley; February); opening of Richard Brinsley Peake's adaptation *Presumption, or, the Fate of Frankenstein* (29 July); publication of 'Giovanni Villani' in *The Liberal* (30 July); Mary returns to London with Percy Florence (25 August); Mary sees Peake's *Presumption* (28 August); second edition of *Frankenstein* published (August); Mary receives small annual allowance of £100 from Sir Timothy Shelley

1824 'On Ghosts' published in the *London Magazine* (March); 'The Bride of Modern Italy' published in the *London Magazine* (April); Byron dies at Missolonghi in Greece (19 April); begins writing *The Last Man*; works on editing Percy's *Posthumous Poems,* to the dismay of Sir Timothy Shelley, who threatens to withdraw her annual allowance, but raises it to £200

1825 Godwin declared bankrupt

1826 Publication of *The Last Man* (Henry Colburn; 26 February); Charles Bysshe Shelley, the son of Percy and Harriet, dies; Percy Florence Shelley becomes heir apparent (14 September); publication of 'The English in Italy' in the *Westminster Review* (October); publication of 'A Visit to Brighton' in the *London Magazine* (December)

1827 Agrees to help Thomas Moore with his life of Byron (published 1830–1)

1828 Begins writing *The Fortunes of Perkin Warbeck* (January); begins writing short stories and poems for *The Keepsake* (March); visits Paris, meets Prosper Mérimée; contracts smallpox (April)

1829 'Illyrian Poems–Feudal Scenes', review of works by Mérimée, published in the *Westminster Review* (January); assists Cyrus Redding in the publication of the Galignani (Paris) edition of Shelley's poems (June–January 1830)

1830 Thomas Moore publishes volume I of his *Letters and Journals of Lord Byron: With Notices of his Life* (January); *The Fortunes of Perkin Warbeck: A Romance* published (Colburn and Bentley; May); composes 'Transformation' for the 1831 edition of *The Keepsake* (Galignani; November–December)

1831 Begins *Lodore* (January); volume II of Moore's *Byron* published; revised edition of *Frankenstein,* with an Author's Introduction, in Bentley's Standard Novels series (Colburn and Bentley; November); 'Transformation' published

1832 Death of William Godwin Jr, son of William and Mary Jane Clairmont Godwin (September); Percy Florence enters Harrow (September)

1833 Moves to Harrow; publication of 'The Mortal Immortal' in *The Keepsake*

1835 Publishes volume I of *Lives of the Most Eminent Literary and Scientific Men of Italy, Spain and Portugal* (Longman); publishes *Lodore* (Richard Bentley; March); publishes volume II of *Lives of . . . Men of Italy, Spain and Portugal* (October)

1836 Removes Percy Florence Shelley from Harrow; relocation to Regent's Park, London (March); death of William Godwin (April)

1837 Publishes *Falkner, A Novel* (Saunders and Otley; February); publishes volume III of *Lives of . . . Men of Italy, Spain and Portugal* (September–October); Percy Florence Shelley enters Trinity College, Cambridge (October)

1838 Sir Timothy Shelley allows the publication of his son's poems with the condition that there is no biographical memoir. (August); Mary Shelley publishes volume I of *Lives of the Most Eminent Literary and Scientific Men of France* (Longman; August)

1839 Publication of four volumes of *Poetical Works of Percy Bysshe Shelley*, with prefaces and notes (January–May); publishes volume II of *Lives of . . . Men of France* (August); one-volume edition of Percy Shelley's *Poetical Works* (Moxon; November); publishes edition of Percy Shelley's *Essays and Letters from Abroad, Translations and Fragments* (Moxon)

1840 Travels to Paris with her son and his friends for a tour of the continent, with travel through Germany, Switzerland and the Italian Lakes (June–September); Percy Florence returns to England (September); Mary Shelley travels to Paris where she remains until December

1841 Returns to London (January); Percy Florence Shelley graduates from Cambridge (February); Mary Jane Godwin dies (June)

1842–3 Undertakes a second trip to the continent with Percy Florence and friends; sees Claire Clairmont in Paris

1844 Death of Sir Timothy Shelley (24 April); Percy Florence Shelley succeeds to the baronetcy and estate. Publication of *Rambles in Germany and Italy in 1840, 1842, and 1843* (Moxon; July)

1845 Attempted blackmail of Mary Shelley by Gatteschi (September); attempted blackmail of Mary Shelley by George 'Byron' (October)

1848 Marriage of Sir Percy Florence Shelley to Jane St John (22 June); complains of headaches

1850 Diagnosis of brain tumour (17 December)

1851 Mary Shelley dies at the age of fifty-three at home in London (1 February). Buried in Bournemouth with her parents, who were exhumed from St Pancras Churchyard at the request of Lady Jane Shelley

Introduction

> It is not singular that, as the daughter of two persons of distinguished literary celebrity, I should very early in life have thought of writing. As a child I scribbled; and my favourite pastime during the hours given me for recreation was to 'write stories'. Still, I had a dearer pleasure than this, which was the formation of castles in the air – the indulging in waking dreams – the following up trains of thought, which had for their subject the formation of a succession of imaginary incidents. My dreams were at once more fantastic and agreeable than my writings.
>
> (Mary Shelley, 'Author's Introduction' to the Standard Novels Edition of *Frankenstein, or the Modern Prometheus*, 1831)

This is a book that seeks significantly to revise our understanding of Mary Shelley's engagement with the Gothic. Whilst acknowledging and exploring the immense significance of *Frankenstein* as it was published in both 1818 and 1831, the study also looks at what Mary Shelley published in between those two editions of *Frankenstein* as an evolution of her preoccupation with Gothic terror and horror. Looking at *Frankenstein*, *Matilda* (1819), *Valperga* (1823), *The Last Man* (1826) and a range of short stories and essays that she published before her 1831 edition of *Frankenstein*, *Mary Shelley* reappraises the astonishing breadth, literary flexibility, curiosity and transformation that characterise the author's engagement with Gothic literary tropes, analysing a broader range of her works than have to date been included in the Gothic canon. In so doing, it argues that in spite of the generic differences between these four major novels and the selected short stories and essays, the themes that emerge in the quintessentially Gothic novel *Frankenstein* remain central to these works that follow. The author's preoccupation with terror and horror, and how to regulate these emotions, furthermore, sharpens in scope and critique as her fictional practice evolves.

Frankenstein, which was not a runaway success when it was first published in 1818, and *Matilda* (1819), which remained unpublished during Mary Shelley's lifetime, are generally regarded as publications that are discrete from Mary Shelley's later works. In 1823, Mary published *Valperga*, a historical romance, and in 1826, she published *The Last Man*, a novel that has been read as science fiction, environmental catastrophe and psychobiography. The writing of over two hundred essays, reviews and short stories sustained Mary Shelley financially in the wake of the death of Percy, pieces that she published in periodicals such as the *New Monthly Magazine* and the *London Magazine*, and in literary annuals such as *The Keepsake*. The initial refusal of her father-in-law, Sir Timothy Shelley, to provide for her and her one surviving child, Percy Florence, had the effect of significantly augmenting his daughter-in-law's prolific creative output. Mary then also published three further novels. *The Fortunes of Perkin Warbeck* in 1830 was a historical novel that addressed a popular subject of historical curiosity, one covered previously by authors such as Baculard d'Arnaud and Sophia Lee, about the famous pretender to the English throne. In 1831, with the publisher Henry Colburn, Mary Shelley issued a new and significantly revised edition of *Frankenstein*, one which carried a new Introduction by her, and which also made some significant changes to the original novel as it was first published in 1818. Two further novels followed, *Lodore* (1835) and *Falkner* (1837), which showed a marked shift towards the domestic sensibilities of the Victorian period.

The received view of the career of Mary Shelley is that it falls broadly into two phases that were divided by the death of her husband Percy Bysshe Shelley in 1822. Tilottama Rajan, for example, in her excellent Introduction to the Broadview edition of *Valperga*, notes:

> Shelley's complex relationship to her literary parents – as well as to Romanticism generally – is at the root of the different ways critics

> have narrativized her corpus. Her career is generally seen as falling into two phases, divided by the death of Percy, and coinciding with a shift from Romanticism to the pre-Victorian 1830s.[1]

Rajan acknowledges that Mary Shelley's interest in the fantastic 'survived', 'encrypted' in the short stories that she composed for *The Keepsake*, but does not read this interest into the other works that she composed before those tales of 1829 and 1831. With the notable exception of an essay by Nora Crook which appeared in Blackwell's *A Companion to the Gothic* (2000), critics who approach the career of Mary Shelley from the perspective of the Gothic tradition also tend to observe this narrative of Mary Shelley's career, focusing on either *Frankenstein* alone, or else including at best the novella *Matilda* that she wrote in 1819 immediately after *Frankenstein*.[2] Of course, there is a good reason for this; in studies of a popular literary form that was used by hundreds of authors, Mary Shelley is one Gothic author among many, and there may be neither space nor time to consider other works. But if we confine ourselves to her early works alone, if we follow the received narrative of her career, I argue, then we as readers of the Gothic risk overlooking the deep veins of connection between her different fictions. The intellectual curiosity that drove those different works, furthermore, did not function in quite the linear way that we imagine. We overlook, for example, the fact that Mary Shelley had begun to consider the plot of her historical novel *Valperga* in 1817, even before the publication of *Frankenstein*. We also miss the fact that just as *Valperga* was finally published in 1823, the adaptation of *Frankenstein* for the theatre in July 1823 suddenly made the author famous.

The fortunes of *Frankenstein* were revived following the runaway success of Richard Brinsley Peake's dramatic adaptation in the play *Presumption, or the Fate of Frankenstein*.[3] In the wake of her move back to England after the death of Percy Bysshe Shelley, Mary undertook a rare excursion to attend the play with her father William Godwin and her friend Jane Williams. 'But lo and behold! I found myself famous!' she wrote to Leigh Hunt.[4] The dramatisation was a resounding success, playing on the audience's emotions and terrors. Victor Frankenstein shrieked 'It lives!' as the monster, performed to great acclaim by T. P. Cooke, vandalised the laboratory of his creator. This was the moment when *Frankenstein, or the Modern Prometheus* assumed the popular mythical status that continues to endure to this day. Cooke's classic performance of the creature ransacking the laboratory, replete with a greenish face and blue body, has since been reinterpreted, most famously by Boris Karloff in James Whale's 1931 classic *Frankenstein*. The popularity of Cooke's performance led to an unusually long run in the theatre. It prompted the financially ever-needy William Godwin to contemplate a second edition of Mary's first novel.[5] Tempting and convenient though it may be to imagine that by this point in 1823 Mary, believing that *Frankenstein* was a commercial failure, had decisively taken another direction in her writing career by composing a historical novel, this is not the case. An author driven by intellectual curiosity, Mary Shelley experimented throughout her literary career with different generic forms as suitable carriers for her anatomisations of human feeling. While there may have been some commercial imperative to her experimentation, her art, like that of her scientist Victor Frankenstein, is driven first and foremost by a selfless curiosity to discover the origins of our feelings of terror and horror.

My argument in this book is that the same myopic vision that conflated the scientist Victor Frankenstein with his nameless creation in the twentieth century has also led to a similar underappreciation of how the Gothic, with its theorisation of terror and horror, permeates the rest of Mary Shelley's work beyond *Frankenstein*. In their edited collection *The Mary Shelley Reader*, Betty T. Bennett and Charles E. Robinson argue that one of the central themes uniting Mary Shelley's *oeuvre* is 'the redemptive value of a broad and humanitarian education', but that this has been underappreciated because we 'interpret the author on limited evidence, frequently on the basis of *Frankenstein* alone.'[6] For Mary Shelley, one of the general values of the 'broad and humanitarian education' that Bennett and Robinson identify lay in its potential to teach its recipients how to manage the experiences of terror and horror. It is a theme, I argue, that we see across all of her works in one form or another, works which, whether they assume the generic contours of historical novels, science fiction or short stories, persistently explore the characters' reactions to emotional extremes. How we deal with those universal emotional extremes, her work tells us, depends on the degrees to which we have been exposed to that broad and humanitarian education to which Bennett and Robinson have referred. A partial, neglected, self-determined education, we discover across her works through the characters of Robert Walton, Victor Frankenstein, the nameless creature (in *Frankenstein*), Castruccio (in *Valperga*) and Lionel Verney (in *The Last Man*), can lead to a weakened ability to confront and manage the omnipresent forces of terror and horror. We all have passions, her works tell us, but how we control those passions is central to whether we become a Promethean overreacher, isolated from society, or a functioning member of a community. And we learn how to control our excesses of emotion through our commitment to that broad, humanitarian education, an education that is not sniffy about its Gothic precedessors such as Ann Radcliffe and Matthew Lewis, but that views authors such as Radcliffe and Lewis as the intellectual and creative equals of Samuel Richardson, Jean-Jacques Rousseau, Madame de Staël and others.

In order to understand that interrelation of the 'humanitarian education' with how the Gothic functions across Mary Shelley's work, it is now necessary to examine in brief her intellectual heritage. As she wrote in her Introduction to the 1831 edition of *Frankenstein*, it 'is not singular that, as the daughter of two persons of literary celebrity, I should very early in life have thought of writing.'[7] As the daughter of Mary Wollstonecraft and William Godwin, Mary had, as she emphasised, a unique and exceptional literary heritage. Her mother, Mary Wollstonecraft, had died in 1797, within days of giving birth to her, from a puerperal fever that might have been preventable with better medical intervention.[8] Married less than a year, Wollstonecraft's death left Godwin with a newly born baby and a stepdaughter Fanny Imlay, who was the offspring of Wollstonecraft's former romance with the American Gilbert Imlay. Godwin, in the wake of this premature bereavement, became, as William St Clair and Emily W. Sunstein observe, an affectionate, but distant father to both Fanny and Mary. He remarried in 1801, having earlier resolved to find another wife. Mary Jane Clairmont was not the first woman that he had attempted to court to become a stepmother to his daughters, but she was the first to accept Godwin's proposal, and she brought with her into the marriage a son, Charles, and a daughter, Jane, who was later to rename herself Claire Clairmont and become, fleetingly, Byron's lover.[9]

Mary Wollstonecraft was author of the globally famous *A Vindication of the Rights of Men* (1790), which had been commissioned in response to Edmund Burke's reactionary *Reflections on the Revolution in France* (1790) and defended the precepts of the revolution in France. Her second major work, *A Vindication of the Rights of Woman* (1792), demanded 'JUSTICE for one half of the human race', arguing in especial detail for the correct and proper education of girls, an education that would extend beyond the frivolities of needlework and the playing of the pianoforte. Later in the 1790s, Wollstonecraft turned to fiction as a method of demonstrating her ideas, composing the novels *Mary* and *The Wrongs of Woman; or Maria*, which, in their dystopian exploration of the consequences of hasty and pecuniary marriages, called for a revision of marital and divorce laws, and another semi-autobiographical work *The Cave of Fancy*. Wollstonecraft's turn to fiction was, no doubt, also influenced by the reviewing that she undertook to sustain herself financially. Amongst other authors, she reviewed *The Italian* by Ann Radcliffe in 1797.[10] Godwin too had cast reverberations across the world with his 1793 *Enquiry Concerning Political Justice*. An enormous work that is hard to categorise, written too in part to argue against reactionaries like Edmund Burke, Godwin's work addressed, among many other concerns, free will, property, marriage, necessity, the power of the mind, education, war and revolution.[11] Like Wollstonecraft's, precepts concerning education that he there espoused, free love and the equal division of property were put into fictional practice with his 1794 novel *Things as They Are, or, the Adventures of Caleb Williams*, which explored the imagined and real terrors of the eponymous servant when he is pursued by his employer, Mr Falkland, after discovering that he has murdered his obnoxious landowning neighbour, Tyrrel. Godwin continued writing fiction throughout his career, and, like his daughter later, experimented with a range of genres that could be described in the same vein as those of his daughter: Gothic, historical, autobiographical and political. It comes as little surprise, then, that Mary Shelley adverted to this heavyweight intellectual heritage as a considerable influence and inspiration on her in the first paragraph of her authorial theorisation of *Frankenstein*. But it was an inheritance that also placed a considerable burden on her. The anxiety of whether she was sufficiently good to follow in her parents' chosen vocations is articulated in the 1831 Author's Introduction to *Frankenstein*. As a child, Mary confesses, 'My dreams were at once more fantastic and agreeable than my writings. In the latter I was a close imitator – rather doing as others had done than putting down the suggestions of my own mind.'[12] The imitation of her early writing, she admits, was substantially different from her dreams, which were hers and hers alone.

This authorial anxiety about originality, creativity and dreaming was pervasive throughout her career, but the evidence that we now have suggests that Mary Shelley's early childhood compositions were strikingly original. As Emily W. Sunstein notes, 'Mary's own writing was first published when she was ten and a half – a feat that she omitted, typically, from her *Frankenstein* Preface.' Godwin, sending to a friend in 1808 the song 'Mounseer Nongtongpaw' that Mary had expanded and remodelled from Charles Dibdin's 1796 musical comedy *The General Election*, proudly observed in his accompanying letter, 'That in small writing is the production of my daughter in her eleventh year.'[13] He went on to publish her song in the same year.[14] Exposed from a young age to the intellectual sociability that characterised her father's household in London's Skinner Street, Mary encountered, among other writers and intellectuals, Samuel Taylor Coleridge, Henry Crabb Robinson and William Wordsworth, a few of the many authors who came to genuflect at the feet of Godwin. Her childhood was characterised by an intellectual excitement, where she attended the theatre, visited art exhibitions and listened to extraordinary philosophical, literary and political conversations. That rarefied education was interrupted during a short period of her adolescence when, because of her strained relationship with her stepmother, she was sent away to stay with the Baxter family on the shores of the River Tay in Scotland (1812–14). But the enforced exile from London was not unhappy: in Scotland she enjoyed the open countryside, the company, a strong friendship with Isabel Baxter, and the different types of sociability that she there encountered. She was taken to Edinburgh, St Andrews and John o'Groats, where she looked across at the Orkney Islands, which she was later to use as a location for both *Frankenstein* and her later novel *The Fortunes of Perkin Warbeck* (1830).

When she returned to London from Dundee in March 1814, Mary was sixteen and a half. There, during the month of May 1814, she met again an acolyte of her father's at Skinner Street, the twenty-one year old married poet Percy Bysshe Shelley. Their courtship was impassioned and rapid; Jane Clairmont, her step-sister, would accompany the two of them as they walked around St Pancras Churchyard, where the body of Mary Wollstonecraft was buried. With the pretext of putting flowers on her mother's grave, Mary contrived to meet Percy there in private. The extent of their infatuation was mutual; Percy Shelley praised both her smile and '[t]he originality and loveliness of Mary's character' in a letter to his friend Thomas Jefferson Hogg, confessing that he found himself 'far surpassed in originality, in genuine elevation and magnificence of the intellectual nature'.[15] Their mutual infatuation moved into a passion with far-reaching consequences, leading to their elopement to the Continent later in 1814, their estrangement from William Godwin and the suicide of Shelley's wife, Harriet Westbrook. What emerges from the correspondence of both is a strong impression that their attraction to each other was founded just as much on intellectual fascination as it was on physical attraction.

The Journals of Mary Shelley, skilfully edited by Paula R. Feldman and Diana Scott-Kilvert in 1987, begin during the year in 1814, the year in which she eloped with Shelley. In Paris, after their elopement to the Continent, Mary and Shelley purchased a green notebook that was to become 'Mary and Shelley's Journal Book'. Recorded at first as a joint enterprise, the journal-keeping persisted in the wake of Shelley's death. In part a record of her tempestuous circumstances as they unfolded throughout her life, it also serves the more functional role of recording the reading that she and Percy Bysshe Shelley undertook throughout their time together. There are columns that record her extensive reading, and columns recording that of Shelley. Those works which were read together are cross-referenced. Thus we discover from these journals the extent to which, during her first year with Percy Bysshe Shelley, the young

Mary Godwin immersed herself in reading some of the most popular examples of the so-called 'first wave' of Gothic fiction that had flourished in the 1790s. On Thursday 22 September 1814, for example, the entry that Jane (later to rename herself Claire) Clairmont made in her journal noted that Mary 'reads the monk all evening' while 'Shelley draws.'[16] She was of course referring to Matthew Lewis's infamous Gothic romance, *The Monk* (1796), which had been subject to the charge of unjustifiably indulging in the extremes of horror in its portrayal of rape, incest, matricide and fratricide.[17] Lewis had not hesitated to expose his readership to the realisation of many scenarios which were implicit in earlier Gothic works such as Horace Walpole's *The Castle of Otranto* (1764) and Ann Radcliffe's *The Mysteries of Udolpho* (1794). Writing for the *Critical Review* in 1797, Samuel Taylor Coleridge had made an interesting and early connection between Lewis's *The Monk* and the prevalent practice of viewing the dismemberment of animals and humans in anatomy theatres:

> Situations of torment, and images of naked horror, are easily conceived; and a writer in whose works they abound, deserves our gratitude almost equally with him who should drag us by way of sport through a military hospital, or force us to sit at the dissecting-table of a natural philosopher [...] Figures that shock the imagination, and narratives that mangle the feelings, rarely discover *genius*, and always betray a low and vulgar taste.[18]

Coleridge's review was written in 1797, the year that Mary Shelley was born, but his comparing of the experience of reading *The Monk* to the enforced horror of sitting 'at the dissecting-table of a natural philosopher' may well have been known to Mary Shelley, given her father's friendship with Coleridge. Coleridge's further judgement on *The Monk,* namely that 'figures that shock the imagination, and narratives that mangle the feelings, rarely discover *genius*', may also have assisted Mary Shelley in deciding to adopt a different narratological approach to her first novel *Frankenstein.* We do not know what Mary Shelley made of *The Monk* when she read it in 1814, but we do know that it is a work that she later referred to in her essay 'On Ghosts', where she advised her readership to 'take up, I beseech you, the story of the Bleeding Nun' at the hour of midnight on a cold, windy night if they wanted to test their belief in ghosts.[19]

Lewis's mode of horror was in distinct contrast to that of Ann Radcliffe, the 'great enchantress', who was the bestselling Gothic novelist of her age. Terror and horror were strongly contested aesthetic categories in the eighteenth century, which became increasingly bound up in the execution and evaluation of the Gothic. Edmund Burke's 1757 *A Philosophical Enquiry into the Origin of our Ideas of the Sublime and Beautiful* connected the aesthetic of terror with the sublime, arguing that 'whatever is in any sort terrible, or is conversant about terrible objects, or operates in a manner analogous to terror, is a source of the sublime.'[20] Ann Radcliffe was well versed in the Burkean sublime, and was celebrated during her lifetime for innovating on the Burkean model. Nathan Drake, a contemporaneous commentator on Radcliffe's art, first foregrounded the necessity of using 'mysterious incidents' in the careful crafting of terror before going on to praise Radcliffe's skill in so doing:

> Terror [. . .] requires no small degree of skill and arrangement to prevent its operating more pain than pleasure. Unaccompanied by those mysterious incidents which indicate the ministration of beings mightier far than we, and which induce that thrilling sensation of mingled astonishment, apprehension and delight so irresistibly captivating to the generality of mankind, it will be apt to create rather horror and disgust than the grateful emotion intended.[21]

Drake went on to praise Ann Radcliffe, calling her the 'Shakspeare [*sic*] of Romance writers' because of her careful 'intermixture' of terrifying scenes with 'beautiful description'.[22] By connecting Radcliffe with Shakespeare, Drake drew a parallel between Shakespeare's 'inventive elegance' in drawing on superstitious imaginings in his great tragedies such as *Hamlet* and *Macbeth*, and Radcliffe's own carefully wrought scenes of terror in her works. He singled out Radcliffe's 1797 novel *The Italian* for especial praise in this context, arguing that 'the attempt of Schedoni to assassinate the amiable and innocent Ellena whilst confined with Banditti in a lone house on the sea shore, is wrought up in so masterly a manner that every nerve vibrates with pity and terror.'[23] Pleasurable terror, for both Drake and Radcliffe, lay in the careful evocation of a scene, the accordant circumstances of time, place and atmosphere that, for example, characterised the appearance of the ghost in *Hamlet*. Drake's argument on the judicious use of terror reappeared with little modification in Ann Radcliffe's own posthumously published essay 'On the Supernatural in Poetry' (1826). There, discussing Shakespeare's use of terror in his tragedies, Radcliffe has two interlocutors debate the respective qualities of terror and horror. After much discussion, they conclude that while horror contracts and freezes the imagination, terror by contrast provides pleasure and imaginative potential. The significance of the posthumous publication of Radcliffe's essay in the *New Monthly Magazine* in 1826, a periodical to which Mary Shelley also contributed later in her career, is something that I explore further in Chapter 5 in relation to the 1831 edition of Shelley's *Frankenstein*.

Mary Shelley was conversant with at least some of the works of Ann Radcliffe before the first publication of *Frankenstein* in 1818. We see from the meticulously recorded reading lists in the journals that Mary read both Radcliffe's *The Mysteries of Udolpho* (1794) and *The Italian* (1797) between the years of 1814 and 1815. On Sunday 27 November 1814, Mary herself recorded in her journal: 'Read the Italian and talk all day – a very happy day indeed.' Then on Monday 28 November, she records, 'Finish the Italian.'[24] Her consumption of *The Italian* was rapid and intensive. Frequently praised as offering a direct response to Matthew Lewis's *The Monk* in its more strained evocation of terror, *The Italian* charts the experiences of a young heroine, Ellena di Rosalba, who is persecuted by the monk Schedoni in the interests of the Marchesa di Vivaldi, who seeks to prevent her son's marriage to Ellena. The scenes where Schedoni haunts and persecutes Ellena are those which Drake singled out for praise when he referred to the novel's magisterial use of terror. Radcliffe's version of Gothic placed fear more firmly in the imaginations of her protagonists: her mode of terror involved anatomising the fear of incest, rape and imprisonment as the young heroine imagines their threats. *The Italian* becomes an exploration of how a heroine might withstand the terrors of her imagination, as Ellena's repeated abductions and imprisonments place her subjectivity under enormous pressure. Like Lewis's *The Monk*, Radcliffe's *The Italian* clearly remained a prominent feature of Mary Shelley's literary imagination, as she has her protagonist, Lionel Verney, in her 1826 novel *The Last Man*, invoke the novel's haunting monk as he wanders through the deserted streets of Rome.

The Monk and *The Italian* were two of many literary works that Mary Shelley recorded reading in 1814. Amongst others, she also read Wordsworth's 1814 poem *The Excursion*, Robert Southey's poems *Madoc* and *The Curse of Kehama*, Shelley's *Queen Mab* (1813), her father's *Things as They Are, or the Adventures of Caleb Williams* (1794), her mother's *Wrongs of Woman*, 'Miss Baillys plays' and Mungo Park's *Travels in the Interior Districts of Africa* (1799).[25] Her reading illustrates just how broad and 'humanitarian' her scope was. Highlights of the 1815 reading list also include a rereading of her beloved and much-cited Milton's *Paradise Lost* (1667), Madame de Staël's *De l'Allemagne* (1810–13), Samuel Richardson's *Clarissa* (1748), Walter Scott's 1814 historical novel *Waverley* and multiple works by Jean-Jacques Rousseau, including his *Confessions* (1782), *Émile ou de l'éducation* (1762) and his espistolary novel of sentiment, *Julie, ou La Nouvelle Héloïse* (1761).[26] Amidst these lengthy reading lists, it is easy to lose sight of the Gothic works that she read, and of the way in which she read them alongside works of philosophy, politics, sentimental literature, Romantic poetry and drama. Nonetheless, the fact that *The Monk* and *The Italian* were both read some sixteen and seventeen years respectively after their first publication, in the years immediately preceding the creation of *Frankenstein* at the Villa Diodati, is, in itself, significant. While many critics tend to look on *Frankenstein* as being 'revisionist Gothic', or the first example of what was viewed as 'the second wave of Gothic', one of the particularly striking things about *Frankenstein* is its ability to consume and transform the Gothic successes of the 1790s.[27] The prefatorial conceit of the discovered manuscript in *The Italian*, derived from the foundational example of Horace Walpole's *The Castle of Otranto*, for example, was a conceit that was invoked in many Gothic romances of the 1790s. Using manuscripts that are barely legible, subject to imperfect translation and possibly mutilated became one of the Gothic's major modes of interrogating whether the novel as a form could address the silences, contradictions and problems within language itself. Mary Shelley was clearly inspired by the conceit of the manuscript, alongside the epistolary practices of Samuel Richardson and Jean-Jacques Rousseau, as she assembled the complex narrative frame of *Frankenstein*. The Promethean ending of Lewis's monk Ambrosio, dashed to death by Lucifer on the rocks and left to be feasted on by the birds, recalls the fate of Prometheus, the demi-god who defied the gods by stealing fire for the benefit of mankind, and was then punished by being chained to the rocks for eternity, while eagles pecked at his liver. Prometheus was also portrayed in William Godwin's pseudonymously published *The Pantheon* in 1806 as a figure whose benevolent intentions were frustrated by the gods.[28] The influence of Prometheus on the works of Byron, Percy Shelley and Mary that emerged from the Summer of 1816 is clear. It is there in the subtitle of *Frankenstein, or the Modern Prometheus*, and made even more explicit in Percy Shelley's dramatic poem *Prometheus Unbound* and Byron's shorter poem 'Prometheus'.

Both Radcliffe and Lewis, read quickly but carefully by Mary Shelley alongside many other works that make their way into her fiction, offered her examples of authorship intent on anatomising evil, unaccountable impulses. Her reading during 1814 and 1815 was an apprenticeship for her subsequent authorship. Much later, in the 1831 Introduction to Colburn's edition of *Frankenstein*, having first traced out her intellectual pedigree from her parents, Mary Shelley adverted to her anxieties concerning 'incapability' as she was challenged to write a ghost story during the Summer of 1816. As E. J. Clery has observed, '[Mary] was threatened not only by immediate comparison with two writers she regarded as great geniuses of the age, but also by the burden of the whole Gothic tradition, now fifty years old.'[29] While the Gothic tradition certainly constituted a redoubtable burden, the synergies of her varied reading in 1814 and 1815, where she read Radcliffe, Lewis and Joanna Baillie alongside so many different types of works, suggested to her ways in which to transform it into a literary inheritance that was new, fresh and subject to endless transformation.

The genesis of *Frankenstein*, one is tempted to argue, lay in the years that preceded the Summer of 1816, when Mary, Percy Shelley and Claire Clairmont rented a house, the Maison Chapuis, close to Byron's rental, the Villa Diodati on Lake Geneva. Claire Clairmont had made the acquaintance of Lord Byron in London during the previous year, and infatuated with him, she accompanied Mary and Percy across the Continent, persuading them to go to Lake Geneva so that she could again meet Byron there. The eruption of Mount Tambora in 1815, as Gillen d'Arcy Wood has recently documented, led to a particularly dark summer:

> The year 1816 remains the coldest, wettest Geneva summer since records began in 1753. That unforgettable year, 130 days of rain between April and September swelled the waters of Lake Geneva, flooding the city. Up in the mountains the snow refused to melt. Clouds hung heavy while the winds blew bitingly cold. In some parts of the inundated city, transport was only possible by boat.[30]

The 'year without a summer', 1816, witnessed the gathering in the Villa Diodati of Mary Godwin (later Shelley), Percy Bysshe Shelley, Claire Clairmont, John Polidori and Lord Byron, and led to collective readings of Samuel Taylor Coleridge's *Christabel* (1816) and a collection of ghost stories called *Fantasmagoriana* (1812). *Fantasmagoriana, ou Recueil d'Histoires d'Apparitions de Spectres, Revenants, Fantômes, etc.* was a French translation by Jean Baptiste Eyriès of German Gothic tales by a number of different authors.[31] In her 1831 account of the creation of *Frankenstein,* Mary Shelley refers to 'the wet ungenial summer' as being instrumental in their resorting to reading this translated collection of ghost stories: 'There was the *History of the Inconstant Lover*, who, when he thought to clasp the bride to whom he had pledged his vows, found himself in the arms of the pale ghost of her whom he had deserted.'[32] Mary's brief account of these tales in her 1831 Introduction differs from that of John Polidori, the physician and occasional lover of Lord Byron, who famously wrote *The Vampyre* during this same summer, but their influence on her fiction has been far more extensive than has previously been allowed for. In 'The Spectre Barber' by J. Musäus, for example, we find a story of epiphany, reform and transformation that seems to anticipate those themes of reform and epiphany in her later works *The Last Man* and 'Transformation'. In

F. Laun's 'The Death Bride' or 'La Morte Fiancée', we find a tale that seems to have informed the characterisation of Lord Ruthven in Polidori's tale *The Vampyre* in its jaded descriptions of cosmopolitan society, but Mary Shelley also makes reference to it in her essay 'On Ghosts'.

The Summer of 1816 has to be one of the most well-documented moments in the history of literary creation. Later, in August, Matthew Gregory Lewis, author of *The Monk* also visited the Villa Diodati. Whereas Mary's journal notes record that she often stayed away from the Villa Diodati while Lewis was there, Percy Shelley and Lord Byron enjoyed his company and had many philosophical discussions with him. As it happened, in fact, as Emily W. Sunstein records, interested observers would gather and speculate about the 'league of incest' that Byron had gathered about him.[33] Ken Russell's 1986 film *Gothic* is one particularly lurid imagining of how the Gothic was not just written about, but actually lived by the party assembled at the Villa Diodati, but there are countless others across different media. Most recently, a children's novel entitled *Strange Star* by Emma Carroll, advertised on its front cover as a 'deliciously Gothic thriller', adds a further fictional mystery to the meeting. Carroll's intriguing and well-researched work joins a burgeoning list of fiction, biographies, documentaries and films about this famous gathering.[34] In the recent fictional resurrections of the Summer of 1816, the mysteries that are unaccounted for between the received accounts of that summer from Mary Shelley and John Polidori, the gaps in their tales, become the impetus for new Gothic mysteries.

As Jerrold E. Hogle has argued, what is important to remember about the gathering during the Summer of 1816 is how the readings of Coleridge's *Christabel* and *Fantasmagoriana* revealed to the Diodati group ways in which to 'radicalise' their uses of the Gothic.[35] This revelation, I would argue, is something that remained with Mary Shelley as a staple throughout her writing career. Much as her return to *Frankenstein* in 1831 in her Author's Introduction might suggest a sole commemoration of the summer of 1816 as the moment of creativity in her writing career, I want to suggest throughout the following five chapters that the incredible diversity of her reading in the years which precede the Summer of 1816, as well as her more careful reading of *Fantasmagoriana* than her account reveals, are important models for her writing as it develops over the course of her literary career.

Furthermore, as I argue in the course of this book, Mary Shelley's fiction frequently places female perspective, editorship and authorship close to its central concerns. This repositioning of female experience, where manuscripts survive and rise to the surface of complex narratives, is something that Mary Shelley learned from the tradition of the Gothic novel, a tradition which she transformed dynamically by interrogating the modes of narrating tales of terror more closely. Terror, historical novel, short stories, essays, poetry: the astonishing breadth and versatility of the work that I have selected to examine from Mary Shelley's writing career exposes in turn the heterogeneous nature of what we now hold together under the term 'Gothic writing'.

Opening up the full canon of Mary Shelley has, to date, been the remit of scholars interested in Romanticism and Shelley scholarship. There, in the wake of Anne K. Mellor's ground-breaking *Mary Shelley: Her Life, Her Fiction, Her Monsters* (1988), a broader perspective of Mary Shelley's writing career has opened up. Superb editions of her work have been published during the past three decades. Under the general editorship of Nora Crook, the Pickering Masters edition of *The Novels and Selected Works of Mary Shelley* has issued a vast amount of her works, including dramas, reviews, essays, short stories and all of her significant works of fiction. The Broadview Press has republished excellent editions of her novels *Valperga*, *The Last Man*, *Lodore* and the third edition of *Frankenstein* in paperback. Three great essay collections in recent decades have also adopted a more holistic approach to her *oeuvre*. *Mary Shelley's Fictions*, edited by Michael Eberle-Sinatra, has assembled essays on her works including *Frankenstein*; the second, *Mary Shelley in Her Times,* edited by Betty T. Bennett and Stuart Curran, also aims to broaden our discussion of her *oeuvre*, including essays on Mary Shelley's editorship as well as her own substantial creative output. The third collection, edited by Audrey Fisch, Anne K. Mellor and Esther Schor, and entitled *The Other Mary Shelley,* tips the balance more radically towards looking at her works beyond *Frankenstein*.

Thanks to these excellent editions and essay collections, for the purposes of this study I have been able to make a more sustained appraisal of the literary career of Mary Shelley, and to question what we, as scholars of the Gothic tradition, risk overlooking if this critical bifurcation of her work persists. Just as many in the twentieth century wrongly conflated the name of Victor Frankenstein with his monstrous creature, so too we risk conflating the author Mary Shelley with *Frankenstein* alone.

I write this book as we approach the bicentenary of the publication of *Frankenstein* in 1818. If at first it seems odd, even anomalous, to publish a book that urges us as readers of the Gothic to read more of Mary Shelley beyond *Frankenstein*, it is not. If anything, it testifies to the endurance of *Frankenstein* for Mary Shelley herself since the creative impulses that lay behind her first novel also, in many different and radical ways, galvanised much of her later writing. While critics acknowledge that the revised 1831 edition of *Frankenstein* witnessed a re-engagement with the Gothic on the part of Mary Shelley, there remains a persistence in separating *Frankenstein*, both through questions of authorship and Gothic thematics, from what came after it. And yet, as I argue in the chapters to follow, what George Levine and U. C. Knoepflmacher have deemed 'the endurance of Frankenstein' lies not just in the endless possibilities that the novel itself throws up for critical interpretation, the endless fascination with the Summer of 1816 in which it was composed or the novel's extensive, inexhaustible afterlives.[36] Its endurance also lies in Mary Shelley's own dynamic, radical and seemingly inexhaustible fascination with it across the span of her career.

Adopting a broadly chronological approach to the *oeuvre* of Mary Shelley, in Chapter 1 I examine the 1818 edition of *Frankenstein*. I then proceed to read the female testimonies that surface in *Frankenstein* into her autobiographical exploration *Matilda* (1819) in Chapter 2, and in her historical novel *Valperga* (1823) in Chapter 3. Chapter 4 examines her essay 'On Ghosts' in relation to her 1826 novel *The Last Man*, where we discover a strong moral lesson, carried over from all of her previous works, about the strategic containment of terror and horror. The aesthetics of terror and horror are then pursued into Chapter 5 as I explore the genesis of her 1831 Author's Introduction to Frankenstein in more detail, alongside the short works of fiction that she composed for *The Keepsake*. In the Conclusion to the book, I turn briefly to address those works that followed the revised edition of *Frankenstein*, *Lodore* and *Falkner*. What, I hope, emerges from my study is a truer picture of Mary Shelley; one that does not diminish in any way her contribution to the development of the Gothic genre, but rather augments the significance of her lifelong fascination with it.

1

Frankenstein, or the Modern Prometheus *(1818)*

> How can I describe my emotions at this catastrophe, or how delineate the wretch whom with such infinite pains and care I had endeavoured to form? His limbs were in proportion, and I had selected his features as beautiful. Beautiful! – Great God! His yellow skin scarcely covered the work of muscles and arteries beneath; his hair was of a lustrous black, and flowing; his teeth of a pearly whiteness; but these luxuriances only formed a more horrid contrast with his watery eyes, that seemed almost of the same colour as the dun white sockets in which they were set, his shrivelled complexion, and straight black lips.
>
> (Mary Shelley, *Frankenstein, or the Modern Prometheus* (1818), p. 40)

As the assembled parts of a newly invented body first convulse, Victor Frankenstein the creator feels only 'breathless horror and disgust'. He lists the hideous parts of his creation in a perversion of Renaissance blazon, adumbrating beautiful parts only to emphasise the horror of the whole. As in Shakespeare's Sonnet 130 ('My mistress's eyes are nothing Like the sun'), flowing black hair and pearly-white teeth are luxuriantly desirable qualities. But whereas Shakespeare's sonnet focuses playfully on negating the overall effect of these attributes in order to emphasise a greater love, Frankenstein's separation of the parts of his creature serves only to express horror, and nothing of the charge of excitement and imagination that characterises the process of the sublime.

Scientific discovery and research, as I will explore more fully further into this chapter, characterised the Romantic period to such an extent as to lead Richard Holmes to call it 'The Age of Wonder'.[1] At first glance *Frankenstein* (1818) offers us a deeply different perspective. Victor Frankenstein's disgust at his nameless creation immediately precipitates us into a realm of horror and death. He compares his creature unfavourably with a reanimated mummy:

> Oh! No mortal could support the horror of that countenance. A mummy again endued with animation could not be so hideous as that wretch. I had gazed on him while unfinished; he was ugly then; but when those muscles and joints were rendered capable of motion, it became a thing such as even Dante could not have conceived. [2]

The effects of horror that Frankenstein notes here somewhat lose their charge as he tethers them so specifically to a particularly superficial realm of aesthetics. Horror becomes harnessed to disfigurement all too quickly, brutally reinforced through such terms as 'hideous' and 'ugly'. This is a value judgement that we, as readers, are incapable of endorsing. It is only when the creature acquires mobility, when it can evade the scopophilic gaze of its creator, that it becomes an object of sublimity, '[A] thing such as even Dante could not have conceived'. Mary Shelley's fascination with Dante's *Inferno*, as we will see, extended throughout her writing career. *Inferno*, she later confided to Leigh Hunt, was 'a poem I can only read bits of – the subject being to me so antipatetica but the Purgatorio and Paradiso – the Poet revels in beauty & joy there to the full as much as in the horrors below.'[3] She appreciated the beauty of Dante's Paradise as much as the horrors in *Inferno* but understood that from the juxtaposition of both sublimity arose. *Frankenstein* participates in this understanding; it offers an investigation into the extremes of our responses to beauty and deformity, the paradox of the sublime that had been explored so fully during the eighteenth century and Romantic period. The sublime of *Frankenstein* is a sublimity that seeks to expose the limitations of story-telling and of language itself as we encounter this incredible creation first and foremost as an object rather than a full subject. It is a version of the sublime that questions the myopic vision of the creator, that challenges his ability even to describe his creation, and that awards equal privilege to the natural and supernatural spheres.

'It is the natural world,' Angela Leighton has argued, 'especially that which gives a promise of the supernatural, which is properly the locus of the sublime.'[4] *Frankenstein* is no exception to this observation. It plays with the liminal spaces that separate the natural from the supernatural world not merely in the external world, but also in the internal worlds of its characters. As Victor Frankenstein knows best, he has created his creature from organic substances – a combination of animal and body parts – and yet he insists, as he brings him to life, on only its inhuman qualities. Frankenstein condemns the creature (rightly, as it transpires) for the murder of his beloved younger brother William on the most spurious of pretexts: '"Nothing in human shape could have destroyed that fair child. *He* was the murderer!"'[5] This realisation dawns on Frankenstein just as he notices his creation 'hanging among the rocks of the nearly perpendicular Mont Salêve'.[6] While Frankenstein remains 'motionless' he considers the being 'nearly in the light of my own vampire, my own spirit let loose from the grave, and forced to destroy all that was near to me'.[7] Vampires and revenants were on the minds of the group assembled at the Villa Diodati during the Summer of 1816, with both Polidori and Byron composing vampiric tales in consequence of the ghost story competition. The vampiric image here that Victor uses first and foremost presupposes his own death as he contemplates the extraordinary mobility of his creation. Fred Botting, remarking on the processes of doubling and reversals in the novel, notes that 'Frankenstein's subjectivity disintegrates, its imagined and vain sovereignty turning into the passions and violence of a gothic villain: creation cedes to destruction, mastery to slavery, unity to monstrosity.'[8] The process of transformation, of Frankenstein losing his self as his creature comes to life, gathers increasing force as the novel progresses. Later, Frankenstein perceives the approach of his creation in the grand surroundings of Mont Blanc. These surroundings owed more than a little to Percy Bysshe Shelley, whose poem 'Mont Blanc' famously cast the mountain as a living part of the 'mind of man'. 'Mont Blanc' was first published as part of the collaborative work by Mary and Percy entitled *History of a Six Weeks' Tour through a Part of France, Switzerland, Germany and Holland: with Letters Descriptive of a Sail round the Lake of Geneva, and of the Glaciers of Chamouni*. Published in 1817, this was a work which Mary compiled from old journal entries and letters that both had written between July and November 1814, detailing the tour of the title. A work of three parts, the first consisted of the journal entries that the pair had written concerning the tour undertaken by them in the company of Claire Clairmont during the summer of 1814, the second of four letters sent from Switzerland in 1816, and the third section consisted of the poem 'Mont Blanc'.[9] As a work of collaboration, it is hard to trace the precise authorial provenance of the first section.

The *History of a Six Weeks' Tour* is a collaborative work whose imaginative potential is carried forward to the scenes in *Frankenstein* that are set among the Alps. We know that Percy edited these particular sections of *Frankenstein* and augmented the descriptions of Mont Blanc.[10] It is interesting to note, then, just how detailed the descriptions of the pines, ravines, jutting rocks and summits are in the novel's second volume. As the mountain comes alive as a dynamic object in chapter II of volume II, Frankenstein observes the 'figure of a man, at some distance, advancing towards me with superhuman speed'.[11] On his approach, however, Frankenstein's bias transforms the creature from 'man', to 'superhuman' and to the 'wretch whom I had created'. It is a chain of signifiers that moves us gradually from the natural to the supernatural. The textured descriptions of Mont Blanc fade into insignificance as he moves into focus, negating as he does so Frankenstein's articulacy and his subjectivity. The creature's approach slowly absorbs all of the imaginative space, consuming, as it does so, the 'life' and 'spirit' of Frankenstein's narrative. Sublimity pulses to the surface of *Frankenstein* almost on almost every page; through the novel's meta-commentary on articulacy and selfhood, through its careful dissection of the scientific debates of the day, through the attention to atmosphere and setting, and through the textured layers of the novel that create further fear, horror and terror as we become increasingly unsure of the truth.

If it seems odd that I began my chapter on *Frankenstein* by analysing Victor's process of creation and rejection, it is because chapter IV, where these scenes occur, is the very place where Mary Shelley first began her novel in June 1816.[12] As she would later recall in the 1831 Preface, she had what Emily W. Sunstein calls a 'waking hypnagogic nightmare' when challenged to write a ghost story by Lord Byron: [13]

> My imagination, unbidden, possessed and guided me, gifting the successive images that arose in my mind with a vividness far beyond the usual bounds of reverie. I saw – with shut eyes, but acute mental vision – I saw the pale student of unhallowed arts kneeling beside the thing he had put together. I saw the hideous phantasm of a man stretched out, and then, on the working of some powerful engine, show signs of life, and stir with an uneasy, half-vital motion. Frightful must it be; for supremely frightful would the effect of any human endeavour to mock the stupendous mechanism of the Creator of the world. His success would terrify the artist; he would rush away from the odious handiwork, horror-stricken. He would hope that, left to itself, the slight spark of life which he had communicated would fade; that this thing which had received such imperfect animation would subside into dead matter, and he might sleep in the belief that the silence of the grave would quench forever the transient existence of the hideous corpse which he had looked on as the cradle of life. He sleeps; but he is awakened; he opens his eyes; behold, the horrid thing stands at his bedside, opening his curtains and looking on him with yellow, watery, but speculative eyes.[14]

Shelley then 'opened' her eyes 'in terror'. In thrall to this hypnagogic nightmare which kept her moving between waking and sleeping, Mary Shelley claims that she conceived *Frankenstein.* Her starting point was the moment of the artist's creation of a new human being. The account that she offers asserts the Romantic ascendancy of the imagination in the way in which she is passively 'possessed' and 'guided' by her imagination. But that very passivity is also endowed with the language of terror in its repetition of 'frightful' and indeed, the way in which Shelley even repeats 'I saw', as if narrating a traumatic event that remains hard to articulate. Whilst the moralistic tone towards the blasphemous scientific endeavour was for commercial and contextual reasons sharper here, invoking 'the Creator of the world' as a censorial presence, it is interesting to note how Victor Frankenstein is called an 'artist' and that his hope that 'imperfect animation would subside into dead matter' is highlighted to such a degree. It is worth bearing in mind, as Andrew Smith has also argued in relation to the passage with which I began this chapter, that we should 'read this moment figuratively, because Mary Shelley wants to stress the failure of an idealistic vision', a vision that could be figured in terms of both science and politics.[15] The failure of this vision is figured here in the ways in which the scientific imagery morphs into a Gothic vision. From the 'spark of life' fading, an image which alluded to the galvanic contexts on which the science of *Frankenstein* was founded, to the organic decomposition of the body subsiding 'into dead matter', we then encounter a language of fear with the hope that 'the grave would quench forever the transient existence of the hideous corpse.' With the grave becoming the active agent in this image, we are precipitated into a different form of figurative language, a form which comes, in part, from graveyard poems such as Robert Blair's *The Grave* of 1743, which apostrophised the grave as the source of imaginative power.[16] Shelley further makes us experience the terrors of 'the pale student of unhallowed arts' acutely as she moves into the present tense to describe the chain of events. Victor 'sleeps', he 'opens his eyes' to encounter the 'yellow, watery, but speculative gaze' of his creation. Victor too experiences a hypnagogic nightmare, and one which bears more than a little resemblance to Henry Fuseli's famous painting of 1781 *The Nightmare*. Mary Shelley was acquainted with Fuseli, both through her mother's famously unrequited infatuation with him, and her father Godwin's continuing friendship with him.[17] In Fuseli's painting, the supine female weighed down by a simian incubus sitting just below her chest is gazed on through the curtains by a horse with bulging, watery eyes. In Shelley's novel, the scene is transposed: a helpless, male artist is gazed on by the watery gaze of his own creation. Both are the same in terms of emotional charge, creating terror and confusion in their blurring of the distinctions between waking and sleeping.

Shelley's 1831 account of her nightmare, then, was a powerful version of Gothic narratology in itself, and one which coerced the reader into sharing the terror of Victor Frankenstein. It drew on the beginning of chapter IV, where Mary Shelley began the novel in 1816:

Henry Fuseli, *The Nightmare* (1871) © Bridgeman Library

> It was on a dreary night of November, that I beheld the accomplishment of my toils. With an anxiety that almost amounted to agony, I collected the instruments of life around me, that I might infuse a spark of being into the lifeless thing that lay at my feet. It was already one in the morning; the rain pattered dismally against the panes, and my candle was nearly burnt out, when, by the glimmer of the half-extinguished light, I saw the dull yellow eye of the creature open; it breathed hard, and a convulsive motion agitated its limbs.[18]

Nature here again morphs into supernature through the careful attention paid to the atmospherics of the 'dreary night' and the 'rain patter[ing]'. Each accordant circumstance is carefully evoked in order to prepare us for the 'convulsive motion'. But this is no ghost; it is a new form of life that Victor Frankenstein tells us that he has laboured for more than two years to create. The attention to the flame of the candle, 'nearly burnt out', also brings to mind the Promethean subtitle of the novel, for Frankenstein, the Modern Prometheus, sheds light on creating new life only in order to extinguish it. '[H]alf-extinguished' and 'nearly burnt out' anticipate the horrified, ambivalent feelings that Victor Frankenstein entertains towards his creation. Frankenstein will continue, after these passages, to produce a further series of horrific designations for his creature, including 'fiend', 'spectre', 'vampire', 'devil' and 'detested form', evading his responsibility to give his creation a definitive name.

'Fiend', 'vampire', 'spectre': three of many in a long chain of signifiers that lead nowhere. Mary Shelley took justifiable care and pride in preserving the namelessness of her creature. When in 1823 she attended a performance of the play of Richard Brinsley Peake's *Presumption; or, The Fate of Frankenstein*, she approvingly observed of the play bill's dash to signify the creature: 'The play bill amused me extremely, for in the list of dramatis personae came, —— by Mr T. Cooke: this nameless mode of naming the un[n]ameable is rather good.'[19] The play's creative approach to the namelessness of the creature met with her approval because the creature is ultimately indefinable. It *is* the sublime in its evasion of rational definition and its resistance to definitive designation. Made, as Victor Frankenstein's account emphasises, of both human and animal body parts, of both organic and inorganic matter, the creature defies our very assumptions about life and death. Gothic literature frequently concerns itself with silences, with the inability to express what one has witnessed: we can think here, for example, of the inarticulacy of Manfred's servants in Horace Walpole's *The Castle of Otranto* as they attempt and fail to describe to their master the ghost that they have just seen. The creature's troubling of these borders between life and death, beauty and deformity, render it the ultimate embodiment of this very Gothic concern.

Just as the creature comes to life, the flickering imagery of the passage above suggests an accordant pessimism. For Anne K. Mellor, this pessimism is due to this being a novel 'about what happens when a man tries to have a baby without a woman' and then refuses to clasp 'his newborn child to his breast in a nurturing maternal gesture', a point about parenting echoed by Evelyn Fox Keller who also argues that '*Frankenstein* is a story first and foremost about the consequences of male ambitions to co-opt the procreative function.'[20] Certainly, these are good modes of interpreting this, and they are borne out by Mary Shelley's careful reading of her own mother's work on parenting in *A Vindication of the Rights of Woman*, her father's work on educating children in *An Enquiry Concerning Political Justice* and of Jean-Jacques Rousseau's earlier educational treatise *Émile, ou de l'éducation*. The creature's lack of nurturing is further echoed in the novel by Victor Frankenstein's complaints about his own father's inattentive attention to his education, and by Robert Walton's complaint that 'it is a still greater evil to me that I am self-educated: for the first fourteen years of my life I ran wild on a common, and read nothing but our Uncle Thomas's books of voyages.'[21] Nonetheless, it is worth bearing in mind that this is a novel that revels in ambivalence, contradictions and uncertainty. *Frankenstein* exposes the arguments for careful nurturing and education, whilst reflecting on the possibilities for self-determination that a comparative lack of restraint offers. It both celebrates and laments the consequences of irresponsible dreaming and creation as it presents to us a creature that, despite its 'horrific' appearance, appears at least to be one of the most eloquent debaters of his age.

Frankenstein further reflects both the horror and the wonder of contemporaneous scientific developments. Percy Shelley's Preface to the 1818 edition immediately foregrounds these contexts by asserting that '[t]he event on which this fiction is founded has been supposed, by Dr Darwin, and some of the physiological writers of Germany, as not of impossible occurrence.'[22] Erasmus Darwin had argued, as Andrew Smith observes, for 'an early theory of evolutionary development which suggested the interconnectedness of all life forms'.[23] Darwin's theory permeates the novel, as Frankenstein pays close attention to the origins of life by examining the 'natural decay and corruption of the human body'.[24] But as he does so, he admits that he is 'animated by an almost supernatural enthusiasm', illustrating the porous boundaries between the realms of the supernatural and the scientific. *Frankenstein*'s exposure of the shortcomings of artistic representation in defining and articulating just how we *feel* stems, in part, from the spirit of scientific enquiry during the Romantic period in which it was composed. Just as her Promethean 'artist' Victor Frankenstein cannot settle on a suitable label for his creature, oscillating as he does between the particularly Gothic nomenclatures of 'wretch' 'vampire' and 'fiend', just as he cannot confront and manage the consequences of his creation, so too the novel as a whole does not make up its mind, definitively, as to precisely how to represent scientific, artistic, exploratory and Promethean adventure. Emily W. Sunstein has argued that whereas to Percy Bysshe Shelley, reading Aeschylus' *Prometheus Bound* in 1817 and composing his lyrical drama *Prometheus Unbound* in 1818, the Greek demi-god represented 'Jove's martyred challenger', to Mary Shelley 'Prometheus was a catalyzer'.[25] 'A natural novelist', Sunstein notes, '[Mary Shelley] liked detail, complexities, perversities, and paradox for themselves, and studying people who differ from herself.'[26] This is something that we can observe in Mary Shelley's engagement with scientific endeavour in *Frankenstein, or the Modern Prometheus*. The continued prominence of the work is due in some measure to the ways in which it represents scientific endeavour. The media continue to keep the novel alive in the press by referring to the 'Frankenstein' effect as scientific innovation in the field of genetics, *in vitro* fertilisation and much more is charted with fear, anxiety and denigration.[27] But such headline-grabbing titles, which aim to criticise scientific innovation, do an injustice to the original novel. As Christa Knellwolf and Jane Goodall have argued, *Frankenstein* partakes in a broader ambivalence to the scientific developments of its day, an ambivalence that Mary Shelley's much-studied William Wordsworth characterised in book 8 of *The Excursion* in 1814.[28] On the one hand, as he contemplated scientific progress, Wordsworth confessed:

> With you I grieve, when on the darker side
> Of this great change I look; and there behold
> Such outrage done to nature as compels
> The indignant power to justify herself;
> Yea, to avenge her violated rights,
> For England's bane.[29]

The 'outrage done to nature' must, suggests Wordsworth, incite vengeance for 'her violated rights'. Nature is cast as the helpless female victim of a male aggressor. Mary Shelley was alert to these gendered implications, producing in *Frankenstein*, as Anne K. Mellor has also observed, a pointed critique of the gendered language of scientific language during the Romantic period.[30] We can read such intent in her characterisation of Victor Frankenstein's violation of nature:

> One secret which I alone possessed was the hope to which I had dedicated myself; and the moon gazed on my midnight labours, while, with unrelaxed and breathless eagerness, I pursued nature to her hiding places. Who shall conceive the horrors of my secret toil, as I dabbled among the unhallowed damps of the grave, or tortured the living animal to animate the lifeless clay? My limbs now tremble, and my eyes swim with the remembrance; but then a resistless, almost frantic impulse, urged me forward; I seemed to have lost all soul or sensation but for this one pursuit. It was indeed but a passing trance, that only made me feel with renewed acuteness so soon as, the unnatural stimulus ceasing to operate, I had returned to my old habits. I collected bones from charnel houses; and disturbed, with profane fingers, the tremendous secrets of the human frame. In a solitary chamber, or rather cell, at the top of the house, and separated from all the other apartments by a gallery and staircase, I kept my workshop of filthy creation; my eyeballs were starting from their sockets in attending to the details of my employment. The dissecting room and the slaughter-house furnished many of my materials; and often did my human nature turn with loathing from my occupation, whilst, still urged on by an eagerness which perpetually increased, I brought my work near to a conclusion.[31]

The 'unrelaxed and breathless eagerness' with which Frankenstein pursues nature 'to her hiding places' are suggestive of sexual excitement, but we come to appreciate the deviance of this excitement when we see where he dabbles. The 'unhallowed damps of the grave' and the torturing of 'the living animal' by 'profane fingers' collectively suggest the irreverence of his curiosity and activity. It is an irreverence that inspires in both the creator and the reader a physical, breathless form of terror. Its transgressive nature is reinforced by the solitude of Frankenstein's workshop of 'filthy creation', separated from the rest of humanity. In its splendid isolation, the workshop becomes a prison just like the tower built by William Beckford's character Vathek (1786), the pleasure-dome of Samuel Taylor Coleridge's Kubla Khan (1816) and the tower represented in Byron's contemporaneously composed dramatic poem *Manfred* (1817).

Victor's profanity, like that of Byron's Manfred, is linked explicitly to his engagement with occult philosophy. The works of Cornelius Agrippa, Paracelsus and Albertus Magnus which Victor devours as a young man are immediately discredited. Agrippa, Paracelsus and Magnus were mystics who, as Andrew Smith observes, 'contributed to sixteenth-century alchemy and sought to discover the elixir of life that would lead to its prolongation'.[32] Coming across his son reading Cornelius Agrippa, we learn from Frankenstein that his father with 'a cursory glance' too casually dismisses Agrippa as 'sad trash' without explaining the reasons why.[33] Frankenstein's reading of the three alchemical philosophers receives further condemnation when he first enters Ingolstadt University. There, with 'fear and trembling', Frankenstein tells his tutor, Monsieur Krempe, of his research. The latter's reaction is unequivocally negative: Victor has 'imbibed' 'nonsense', 'exploded systems' and 'useless names'.[34] The relative value of reading such philosophy is assessed in the novel, with Frankenstein's other university tutor, Monsieur Waldman, acknowledging that these philosophers hold some value.[35] But of greater interest is the reaction of Frankenstein to anyone who challenges his reading. Reacting to his father's 'cursory' condemnation of Agrippa, Frankenstein remarks that had his father taken the time, 'It is even possible, that the train of my ideas would never have received the fatal impulse that led to my ruin.'[36] On the one hand, this is good educational advice, derived from Mary Shelley's careful thinking about education. Nevertheless, Frankenstein's 'fatal impulse' can only be ascribed to him and him alone. The phrase 'fatal impulse' emphasises how feeling always comes first for him. The same is true of his reaction to Monsieur Krempe's dismissal of his reading. Krempe takes more time than his father, providing him with a more appropriate reading list, but Frankenstein remarks that 'I did not feel much inclined to study the books that I procured at his recommendation. M. Krempe was a little squat man, with a gruff voice and repulsive countenance; the teacher, therefore, did not prepossess me in favour of his doctrine.'[37] Ascribing his aversion to Krempe to a physiological, instinctual reaction gives the reader a strong insight into a fatal flaw within the character of Frankenstein. Relying on the visual as a shaky index to feeling, Mary Shelley suggests, is always already a fallacious enterprise. Frankenstein's reaction here anticipates his later reaction to his creation, quoted as the epigraph to this chapter, where the horrors of physical repulsion far outweigh any rational consideration of his creature. When, in the sublime setting of Mont Blanc, Frankenstein finally agrees to meet with his creation, he is visually overwhelmed. '"Begone! Relieve me from the sight of your detested form,"' he brutally orders. His creature understands the reasoning behind Frankenstein's reaction better than he does: '"Thus I relieve thee, my creator," he said, and placed his hated hands before my eyes which I flung from me with violence; "thus I take from thee a sight which you abhor."'[38]

Frankenstein's engagement with alchemical philosophy does not imply any outright condemnation of science on Mary Shelley's part. What she probes instead are the measures by which her characters react to what they read and absorb around them. Whereas on the one hand Frankenstein admits that the dreams he entertains, fuelled by devouring the alchemical works of Paracelsus, Magnus and Agrippa remain 'undisturbed by reality', on the other hand he is drawn towards '[t]he natural phaenomena that take place every day before our eyes'.[39] During adolescence, Frankenstein recalls witnessing the devastation that a thunderstorm wreaks on a tree, 'reduced to ribbands of wood' by lightning:

> The catastrophe of this tree excited my extreme astonishment; and I eagerly inquired of my father the nature and origin of thunder and lightning. He replied, 'Electricity;' describing at the same time the various effects of that power. He constructed a small electrical machine, and exhibited a few experiments; he made also a kite, with a wire and string, which drew down that fluid from the clouds.[40]

This account is no doubt taken, as Marilyn Butler notes, from Benjamin Franklin's 1752 experiment with a kite, in which he set out to prove that he could harness electricity. But in Shelley's text, the passage demonstrates Frankenstein's equal investment in modern forms of scientific experimentation with the observation that the kite 'drew down that fluid from the clouds'.[41] The excitement felt by Frankenstein in this experimentation 'completed the overthrow', he records, of Agrippa, Magnus and Paracelsus. Immediately after this, however, Frankenstein again notes an abrupt and unaccountable change to his resolution: 'by some fatality I did not feel inclined to commence the study of any modern system.'[42] The novel yet again underscores how human emotion is more fundamental to its plot than scientific enlightenment, ascribing Frankenstein's failure to engage with 'any modern system' to disinclination and fatality. Frankenstein suggests, here as elsewhere, that 'The different accidents of life are not so changeable as the feelings of human nature.'[43] The emphasis on the unpredictability of feeling brings the novel firmly within the Gothic orbit of exploring the unnameable, inexpressible and contradictory impulses of human nature.

Feeling, and the quest for the human soul, also came increasingly and questionably within the orbit of scientific scrutiny during the Romantic period. The representation of Frankenstein's research into the working of electricity draws on some of the most controversial scientific theories of the day, some of which also attempted to navigate the uncharted territory of emotions and indeed, the human soul. In *The Excursion* Wordsworth alluded indirectly to these scientific discoveries, noting 'almost a soul / Imparted – to brute matter':

> Yet do I exult,
> Casting reserve away, exult to see
> An intellectual mastery exercised
> O'er the blind elements; a purpose given,
> A Perseverance fed; almost a soul
> Imparted – to brute matter. I rejoice,
> Measuring the force of those gigantic powers
> That, by the thinking mind, have been compelled
> To serve the will of feeble-bodied man.[44]

Wordsworth's exultation in 'intellectual mastery' over 'brute matter' both surprises and discomforts him. It is recorded in the hesitation that it is 'almost a soul / Imparted' and by the pause between the verb 'Imparted' and the indirect object 'brute matter'. It further lurks in the begrudging 'Yet' with which he admits his admiration. Such prosodic marks of trepidation illustrate the giddy combination of confusion and excitement that greeted the major scientific debates and discoveries of the period.

Mary Shelley's responses to these developments were on the same emotional spectrum as those of Wordsworth. In her 1831 Preface, Shelley referred to the discussions that took place at the Villa Diodati during the Summer of 1816 on 'the nature of the principle of life, and whether there was any probability of its ever being discovered and communicated'.[45] As Maurice Hindle first pointed out, in her exploration of the paradoxes that lie behind the potential benefits and drawbacks to scientific endeavour, Mary Shelley no doubt drew on the 'voice of the "real" scientist', Humphry Davy, a chemist 'whom Percy Shelley revered'.[46] At the age of fourteen, in 1812, observes Richard Holmes, Mary accompanied her father Godwin 'to hear Humphry Davy give his public lectures on chemistry at the Royal Institution'.[47] She further recorded in her journal reading Davy's 1812 publication *Elements of Chemical Philosophy* between 28 October and 4 November 1816.[48] In the gendered language that Mellor has noted, Davy there charted the ambitions and enthusiasms of science:

> Science has [...] bestowed on [man] powers which may be called almost creative; which have enabled him to change and modify the beings surrounding him, and by his experiments to interrogate nature with power, not simply as a scholar, passive and seeking only to understand her operations, but rather as a master, active with his own instruments [...] who would not be ambitious of becoming acquainted with the most profound secrets of nature; of ascertaining her hidden operations; and of exhibiting to man that system of knowledge which relates so intimately to their own physical and moral constitution? [49]

Adopting a rhetorical approach that brooked no disagreement, Davy noted the spirit of scientific enquiry of the age, a spirit which assumed that everyone would be as enthusiastic as he in seeking out the origins of life. Davy was a poet and chemist whose hallucinatory experimentations with nitrous oxide showed to him the possibility of alternative visions of reality, and whose research on electricity demonstrated its transformative capacities. His experimentations, which he reported in his Bakerian lectures for the Royal Institute (1806), pushed the boundaries of scientific discovery, even at the expense of making himself unwell through his experimentation with nitrous oxide, in the pursuit of knowing better the human 'physical and moral constitution'.[50] Davy's ambition to probe the components of the moral as well as physical constitution was a Promethean task.

The disquiet that augmented around the jurisdiction of Davy's ambitions was in some measure due to the dissection-table research into galvanism carried out by Giovanni Aldini. His uncle Luigi Galvani's *The Effects of Artificial Electricity on Muscular Motion* (1792) had demonstrated to the world how a frog's legs could continue to contract after death and dissection following the application of an electric current. Aldini took this research further, experimenting on the severed heads of criminals in London: after applying an electric current to the 'decapitated criminals', Aldini noted 'strong contractions in the muscles of the face, which were contorted in so irregular a manner that they exhibited the appearance of the most horrid grimaces. The action of the eye-lids was extremely striking.'[51] This is the scientific experimentation that in part informs the creation of the creature in *Frankenstein*: composed of both animal and human body parts that Victor Frankenstein collects from charnel and slaughter houses, the creature's origins are multiple. They are assembled and brought to life in an unethical manner, to say the least.[52]

The fight for the soul as well as the physical body was taken up again in 1816 in a furiously debated row on the ethics of such science. The vitalism debate was sparked between two scientists known to Percy and Mary Shelley; John Abernethy and William Lawrence. The latter served as physician to Percy Bysshe Shelley between 1816 and 1818; the former, Abernethy, was 'a pious, plain-spoken Scot' raised in the Calvinist Church who, in the wake of his mentor John Hunter's speculations about a Life Force that would 'somehow be associated with spontaneous motions inherent in the human physiology', began to form a semi-mystical theory of the source of human life.[53] As Richard Holmes explains:

> Blood itself could not explain life, though it might carry it. This universal 'vitality' was a 'subtle, mobile, invisible substance, super-added to the evident structure of muscles, or other form of vegetable and animal matter, as magnetism is to iron, and as electricity is to various substances with which it may be connected.' Abernethy further suggested that this theory brought scientific evidence – if not exactly proof – to the theological notion of the soul. If the Life Force was 'super-added', some power outside man must obviously have added it.[54]

First the follower of Abernethy, William Lawrence became his adversary in this debate as he denied in clear terms the scientific evidence for the existence of the soul. Lawrence viewed life instead merely as the operational function of the human body. The conservative *Quarterly Review* was outraged by Lawrence's audacity, questioning what, precisely, Lawrence wanted its readership to believe. Shocked that Lawrence proposed that the characteristics of human nature were little more than 'an orang-outang or an ape', the author wondered at the preposterous nature of the claim 'That all the eminent powers of reason, reflexion, imagination, and memory – the powers which distinguish a Milton, a Newton, and a Locke, – are merely the function of a few ounces of organized matter called the brain!'.[55]

While the Shelleys were friends of Lawrence, as recorded in Mary Shelley's journal by the numerous visits that Percy Shelley paid to William Lawrence, *Frankenstein* explores the contours of this vitality debate. As the novel shows the natural consequences of the science, the creation of an artificially-assembled creature, sutured from animal and human body parts, it also shows a new being who, in spite of no nurturing, is capable of language acquisition, knowledge and fine republican feelings. Finely tuned by Mary Shelley's careful following of the vitality debate, alongside her reading of, amongst others, the authors that the *Quarterly* highlighted as distinguishing men from beasts (Milton, Newton and Locke), the Gothic nature of the novel becomes increasingly clear as it seeks to explore the uncharted elements of human character, the space where a soul might reside. *Frankenstein* becomes a novel above all else that concerns itself with origins; the origins of life, the origins of feeling, the sources of manuscript accounts, the novel's relationship to its literary antecedents, the individual's relationship with the textual sources that it reveres, and the much, much larger question of literary authority.

In probing the origins of feeling, Mary Shelley draws attention to the fundamental distinction between feeling something, and acting on that feeling. This is reflected in the novel's engagement with its literary antecedents. *Frankenstein* is inaugurated with an epigraph from book X of Milton's *Paradise Lost* where Adam challenges his father/creator,

> Did I request thee, Maker, from my clay
> To mould Me man? Did I solicit thee
> From darkness to promote me?[56]

With such an opening, the novel immediately raises open-ended questions about origins, creation and duty. The analogies to *Paradise Lost* pervade *Frankenstein*, focusing on the triangular relationship between Adam, God and Satan. In the various permutations of the relationships between these three, Milton's *Paradise Lost* had opened up questions about the Bible's representations of rebellion, filial duty and paternal duty. As Lisa Vargo observes, these were questions that Romantic readers such as William Blake and Percy Shelley had viewed as 'a critique of religion as being responsible for tyranny in contrast to human accountability'.[57] *Frankenstein*'s epigraph from Book X immediately lays out the clear ethical challenge to its readership about the right of one individual to create another, to 'mould Me man'. There can be no mistake in how we map this particular challenge onto the characters in the novel. But less clear is how we should respond to this: the unanswerable question that Adam poses to God remains unanswered in *Frankenstein* because it is, in the context of the Romantic period's scientific innovation, unanswerable.

The creature is the most voracious reader in the novel, apprehending the universe through the selective reading that he comes across when taking shelter in the shed adjoining the De Lacey cottage. He both listens to others reading, such as Felix reading Volney's *Ruins of Empire* (1791) to Safie, and learns to read himself by reading Goethe's novel *The Sorrows of Young Werther* (1774),

Plutarch's Lives (*c.* AD 120) and Milton's *Paradise Lost*. The creature observes of his readings that 'They produced in me an infinity of new images and feelings that sometimes raised me to ecstasy, but more frequently sunk me into the lowest dejection.'[58] While on the one hand such a reaction emphasises an excited absorption with reading, on the other its emotional extremes are troubling, since the sources that he reads, deliberately derived from different genres and centuries, are read indiscriminately in terms of his emotions. As the creature's reading of *Paradise Lost* as a 'true history' emphasises, there is a considerable risk attendant on attempting to work out which character from one text serves as the best analogy from a character from *Frankenstein*:

> 'But *Paradise Lost* excited different and far deeper emotions. I read it, as I had read the other volumes which had fallen into my hands as a true history. It moved every feeling of wonder and awe, that the picture of an omnipotent God warring with his creatures was capable of exciting. I often referred the several situations, as their similarity struck me, to my own. Like Adam, I was created apparently united by no link to any other being in existence; but his state was far different from mine in every other respect. He had come forth from the hands of God a perfect creature, happy and prosperous, guarded by the especial care of his creator; he was allowed to converse with, and acquire knowledge from beings of a superior nature: but I was wretched, helpless and alone. Many times I considered Satan as the fitter emblem of my condition; for often, like him, when I viewed the bliss of my protectors, the bitter gall of envy rose within me.'[59]

Frankenstein's creation here admits to difficulty in establishing whether Adam or Satan is a better metaphor for his condition. Adam too is a singular creation, unique on earth with no apparent ties. However, his creator has provided him with a secure place of habitation with all of his needs provided for, and has taken care to provide him with a companion so that Adam is happy. The creature notes this as he reproaches Frankenstein: 'Remember, that I am thy creature: I ought to be thy Adam; but I am rather the fallen angel, whom thou drivest from joy for no misdeed.'[60] Despite Adam being provided with a companion, he nonetheless reproaches God for creating him in book X of *Paradise Lost,* just as the creature is then permitted to make a supplication to Victor Frankenstein. 'I remembered Adam's supplication to his creator; but where was mine? he had abandoned me, and, in the bitterness of my heart, I cursed him.'[61] There is, however, a danger attendant here, one that is also borne out by the reading undertaken by Victor Frankenstein and Robert Walton. The creature himself observes that 'As I read [. . .] I applied much personally to my own feelings and condition.'[62] His introspective approach to reading is characteristic of what Graham Allen calls a 'radical subjectivism'.[63] There is no referent to external reality as he moves haphazardly between the assortment of works that he comes across. The same also holds true for the 'enthusiasm' with which Frankenstein confesses to having read Cornelius Agrippa, and the way in which Robert Walton characterises his own movement between a history of sea voyages from his Uncle Thomas's library and the poetry of Homer and Shakespeare. In one paragraph, the sea voyages, Walton confesses, create an ardent desire to become an adventurer, but '[t]hese visions faded when I perused, for the first time, those poets whose effusions entranced my soul, and lifted it to heaven. I also became a poet.'[64] The volatility in his purpose, seeing in each work that he reads his future vocation, is mirrored in that of Frankenstein's oscillation between alchemy and natural philosophy, and the creature's application of each character's condition to his own.

The only characters in *Frankenstein* who escape from such 'radical subjectivity', in fact, are those who are touched on in the most tangential ways. Frankenstein's dear companion Henry Clerval, for example, who later falls victim to the creature, is described as a 'boy of singular talent and fancy' whose favourite study is in 'chivalry and romance'. Compared by some critics to Percy Bysshe Shelley, the fact that he 'wrote a fairy tale' at the age of 'nine years old', almost precisely the same age that Mary Shelley wrote her first tale, also places him close to the author herself. Clerval becomes an active author at a young age, putting his dreams into practice by performing plays that he has written with Frankenstein. The distinction here, then, lies in the degrees of dreaming: by composing and performing plays, Clerval observes the distinction between reality and his tales of chivalry. This becomes even clearer when we consider what Frankenstein says of his beloved cousin Elizabeth Lavenza, who is also sacrificed to the vengeance of the creature on her wedding night. She too is an artist, and Frankenstein goes into considerable detail about how they are taught to become enthusiastic about their learning. Such detail reveals the significance of the distinctions in how he and Elizabeth approach their passions:

> Our studies were never forced; and by some means we always had an end placed in view, which excited us to ardour in the prosecution of them. It was by this method, and not by emulation, that we were urged to application. Elizabeth was not incited to apply herself to drawing, that her companions might not outstrip her; but through the desire of pleasing her aunt, by the representation of some favourite scene done by her own hand.[65]

Frankenstein begins with the plural possessive here, emphasising that '[their] studies' are explicitly not about 'emulation'. However, he swiftly moves to the third person, discussing only Elizabeth's application of these precepts, noting that Elizabeth did not draw to be the best, 'but through the desire of pleasing'. There is a subtle distinction here, a distinction that can be applied to the three male transgressors of the novel, Robert Walton, Victor Frankenstein and the nameless creature: all of three of them 'emulate' what they read, whereas Henry Clerval and Elizabeth Lavenza remain able to make the distinction between artistic representation and reality. Henry and Elizabeth are no less artists than Frankenstein. Like the female heroines of Ann Radcliffe, they write poetry, paint and read a lot. In spite of their comparative textual dismissal, called on as they are only when Frankenstein needs them, Henry and Elizabeth are able to take a healthier attitude to their readings. They can 'represent' artistic scenes, plays and poems without perceiving the flawed need to *become* the characters from the books that they read, and the images that they create. This is a consequence of Mary Shelley's own careful and enormously varied reading, and what Sunstein, as I noted above, calls her interest 'in studying people who differ from herself'.[66] Mary Shelley herself knew the dangers and the pleasures inherent in reading, noting as she did of her childhood in the later Author's

Introduction of 1831 that 'my dreams were all my own; I accounted for them to nobody', whereas '[i]n [writing] I was a close imitator – rather doing as others had done than putting down the suggestions of my own mind.' This is how she accounts for the distinctions that she forges as a child between dreaming and writing; dismissing the latter as a child because she can only imitate, or 'emulate'.

A suspicion of emulation permeates *Frankenstein*. This may, at first glance, appear paradoxical: its subtitle, after all, is named after Aeschylus' doomed hero, and its coldly formal dedication 'To William Godwin, author of *Political Justice*, *Caleb Williams*, *etc.*' suggests a desire for approval from the 'sententious and authoritative' father whom, U. C. Knoepflmacher notes, Mary Shelley 'admired and deeply resented' and who oversaw all of her work during his lifetime.[67] Even its first 1818 Preface, in its citation only of classical sources, its numerous references to Romantic poetry, and its privileging of poetry over prose in too apologetic a manner, and in fact written by Percy Bysshe Shelley, as Mary Shelley was later to confess, seems to 'emulate' in its approving citation of '*The Iliad*, the tragic poetry of Greece, – Shakespeare, in *The Tempest* and *Midsummer Night's Dream,* and most especially Milton'. This Preface apologetically relegates the attempts of 'the humble novelist' to a position considerably below these 'highest specimens of poetry', complaining in Wordsworthian fashion of 'the enervating effects of the novels of the present day'.[68] But even if the Preface is written by another, it nonetheless contains the seeds of departure that were so critical to Mary Shelley's Gothic. Speaking of 'the truth of the elementary principles of human nature', the author confesses that 'I have not scrupled to innovate on their combinations.'[69] *Frankenstein* makes its mark in the ways in which it responds critically to scientific innovation, to enlightenment, canonical and Gothic traditions. In so doing, it anatomises the feelings and reactions of its characters to those developing new creative paths.

To combine different traditions, for Mary Shelley, was to innovate a new form of Gothic. Milton is a constant and favourite author of Mary Shelley, an author whom she reads both alone and with Percy Bysshe Shelley. In *Areopagitica*, his published speech in defence of the liberty of the English press, Milton had affirmed his faith in the sanctity of individual judgement, advising his audience: 'Read any book what ever comes to thy hands, for thou art sufficient to judge aright, and to examine each matter.'[70] Mary Shelley clearly shared Milton's faith, for *Frankenstein* slowly evolved into a complex, multi-layered tale which forces us to question and judge the actions of its characters. It anatomises the feelings and extreme reactions of its main protagonists to the range of works that they read and act on. Sir Walter Scott was the first to identify this in his review of the anonymously published novel for *Blackwood's Magazine*:

> A more philosophical and refined use of the supernatural in works of fiction, is proper to that class in which the laws of nature are represented as altered, not for the purpose of pampering the imagination with wonders, but in order to shew the probable effect which the supposed miracles would produce on those who witnessed them. In this case, the pleasure ordinarily derived from the marvellous incidents is secondary to that which we extract from observing how mortals like ourselves would be affected by scenes like these which, daring to depart from sober truth, are still true to nature.[71]

Praising the novel as carrying a 'more philosophical and refined use of the supernatural', what Scott rightly foregrounded was the novel's central interest which lay not so much in those 'supposed miracles' of science, but in 'observing how mortals like ourselves would be affected by scenes like these'.[72]

It was in late 1816 or early 1817 that Mary Shelley added an extra frame to the tale in the form of the correspondence between Robert Walton, a young ambitious explorer who wishes to discover the North-West Passage, a passage which was the subject of much fervent debate and speculation in 1817. In the *Quarterly Review*, which Mary includes in her reading list for 1817, a review appeared of the '*Narrative of a Voyage to Hudson's Bay, in his Majesty's Ship Rosamond*' by one Lieut. Chappell. The substantial review of twenty-four pages began by dismissing the travelogue outright, commenting that in the eight-volume work, 'there is literally nothing worth communicating to the public at large.' The reviewer, one John Barrow who reviewed all of the *Quarterly*'s travel works, spent the remaining twenty-three pages of the review attempting to argue that the North-West Passage had been freed up by the earlier eruption of Mount Tambora:

> Among the changes and vicissitudes to which the physical constitution of our globe is perpetually subject, one of the most extraordinary, and from which the most interesting and important results may be anticipated, appears to have taken place in the course of the last two or three years, and is still in operation. The convulsion of an earthquake and the eruption of a volcano force themselves into notice by the dismay and devastation with which, in a greater or lesser degree, they are almost always attended; but the event to which we allude has been so quietly accomplished, that it might have remained unknown, but for an extraordinary change which a few intelligent navigators remarked in the state of the arctic ice, and the reports of the unusual quantities of this ice observed in the Atlantic.[73]

Barrow's articles for the *Quarterly* insisted on the possibility of this North-West Passage because of the disappearance of the whole, or 'greater part' of an 'impenetrable barrier of ice' off the eastern coast of Greenland. In effect, he was rousing the ambitions of British explorers in his pieces so that one or more of them would set sail and confirm his hypotheses, scorning anyone who had the temerity to deny the disappearance of the barrier of ice. Robert Walton, Mary Shelley's correspondent who frames the novel, is just such a Promethean explorer. He states to his sister that he will 'satiate [his] ardent curiosity with the sight of a world never before visited, and may tread a land never before imprinted by the foot of man'.[74] Privileging his dreams, he insists that 'it ever presents itself to my imagination as the region of beauty and delight' where 'the sun is forever visible.'[75] As Adriana Craciun has observed, '[h]is language reflects experienced Arctic explorers' such as the Elizabethan John Davis, who also framed the Arctic in similarly utopian terms.[76] More broadly, Walton's love of poetry leads him to quote, rather prophetically, directly from Coleridge's 'Rime of the Ancient Mariner' – 'I am going to unexplored regions, to "the land of mist and snow;" but I shall kill no albatross, therefore do not be alarmed with my safety.'[77] But Walton's imaginative engagement goes even further than direct quotation, suturing his letter-writing with other images from Coleridge, such as his reference to 'sailing over a calm sea' in his first letter.[78] His reading and reproduction of Coleridge can be read as dangerously undiscerning since it neutralises the terrifying charge of Coleridge's original. As such, Walton's textual consumption anticipates that of Frankenstein and his creature.

Speaking in terms that explicitly anticipate the Promethean ambitions of Frankenstein, Walton advises his sister, 'You cannot contest the inestimable benefit which I shall confer on all mankind to the last generation, by discovering a passage near the pole to those countries.'[79] The friendship that he recounts as unfolding between him and Victor Frankenstein, who boards his ship in the wake of being pursued by his creature, is one of kinship and of ambition. On the one hand, Frankenstein seems on their first meeting to warn Walton against his Promethean enterprise: 'You seek for knowledge and wisdom, as I once did; and I ardently hope that the gratification of your wishes may not be a serpent sting to you, as mine has been.' But as these letters continue after Frankenstein has recounted his extraordinary tale of caution, they reveal that the cautionary advice is hollow. As Walton's men threaten mutiny due to starvation and poor conditions, Frankenstein rouses himself from his torpor to reproach them:

> [Frankenstein's] eyes sparkled, and his cheeks flushed with momentary vigour. Turning towards the men, he said – What do you mean? What do you demand of your captain? Are you then so easily turned from your design? Did you not call this a glorious expedition? And wherefore was it glorious? Not because the way was smooth and placid as a southern sea, but because it was full of dangers and terror [...] You were hereafter to be hailed as the benefactors of your species; your name adored, as belonging to brave men who encountered death for honour and the benefit of mankind [...] Oh, be men, or be more than men [...] Return as heroes who have fought and conquered, and who know what it is to turn their backs on the foe.[80]

This speech, which Walton records he spoke 'with an eye so full of lofty design and heroism', fortunately has no effect on the intent of the sailors to return, and thus Robert Walton's hopes of glory, at least, are dashed.

But amidst this particularly male version of heroics, there is something more interesting in operation, and that is indicated by the small annotation at the beginning of that letter, 'Walton, in continuation'. Who writes this, and why does it matter? We know from Mary Shelley's journal that in 1815 she had been reading Samuel Richardson's epistolary masterpiece *Clarissa, or the History of a Young Lady*, first published in 1748.[81] The story of the rebellious, doomed young heroine clearly caught her imagination, but more importantly, the epistolary framework of *Clarissa*, as well as so much of Rousseau's eighteenth-century work that she had also been studying, was an object of fascination for her. For, as Fred Botting remarks, with the opening letters of *Frankenstein*, 'the eighteenth-century reader is invoked.'[82] The novel opens with a series of four letters addressed from the explorer Robert Walton to the silent addressee Mrs Saville. We learn in the second sentence of the novel, and of Letter I, that Mrs Saville is Walton's 'dear sister', but only after Walton has first noted that his sister has regarded his enterprise 'with such evil forebodings'.[83] This is in fact the only thing that we learn of Mrs Saville's feelings. Walton's letters continually emphasise feeling and want, but the question that he poses to his sister Margaret in that very first letter, 'Do you not understand this feeling?' is swiftly supplanted by assertions of what Walton wills her to feel and think: 'you cannot contest,' he pleads at one point. Mrs Saville, however, remains silent throughout *Frankenstein*. Never responding, we learn of nothing but the 'evil forebodings' that are mentioned in the very first sentence, which appear to construct her as a character who relies on instinctual feeling. If, however, the creature and Frankenstein, as I have argued, display this 'instinctual feeling' where they act on their emotions, rather than attempting to understand them, we do not get this impression of Mrs Saville. As the opening letters unfold, we learn from Walton that it is his own irrationality that he fears: he 'greatly' needs a friend to help to 'regulate' his mind, he informs Margaret in Letter II, and in Letter III he tries to convince her that he 'will be cool, persevering, and prudent'.[84] Walton's expositional letters demonstrate that he is not fixed in his purpose; that his mind is too receptive, too suggestible to the influence of what he reads at the time.

Anne K. Mellor was the first critic to identify the link between the initials of Mrs Saville (MWS for Margaret Walton Saville) with the initials of Mary Shelley herself, since this part of the story was probably completed after the quiet nuptials of Percy and Mary Shelley in December 1816.[85] The use of those initials is in part a tribute to Mary Shelley's mother.[86] Wollstonecraft haunts the debates on education and reading that I have foregrounded in my discussion. She also lurks implicitly in the theme of the absent mother as Frankenstein seeks to usurp the procreative function. Furthermore, she provides the lifeblood of the Gothic critique that lurks in the silences at the heart of *Frankenstein.* In a section entitled 'Parental Affection' of her 1792 work *A Vindication of the Rights of Woman*, Wollstonecraft argues that 'To be a good mother a woman must have sense, and that independence of mind which few women possess who are taught to depend on their husbands.'[87] Walton's pleading for his silent sister's approval suggests, at least, that this silent addressee has that 'independence of mind' that Wollstonecraft advocated.

Aurally, in French (the language spoken by the De Lacey family), Mrs Saville's name also resembles another silent female character in the novel, that of Safie, whose letters are collected by the creature at the very heart of the novel, and then transmitted to Victor Frankenstein who in turn passes them to Walton. These are then collated and curated by Mrs Saville. Safie, the daughter of a Turkish merchant who betrays Felix, explicitly rejects the oppression of women offered by the religion that her father follows. She flees the patriarchal home in Turkey to seek Felix and his family in Switzerland. As a traveller who rejects her father's injunctions, Safie is for Anne K. Mellor the 'incarnation of Mary Wollstonecraft in the novel'.[88] Providing strong testimonies of a woman being able to choose and judge for herself, Safie's letters offer the traces of a strong female role model, one that is silently supported by Margaret Walton Saville (MWS).[89] The creature notes the importance of Safie's letters, as she 'found means to express her thoughts'. The articulation of these thoughts on patriarchal repression are of course significant, but of equal importance is the fact that they provide the only testimony in the novel that 'will prove the truth' of the creature's 'tale'.[90] Safie labours, in a foreign language, to produce letters that tell of her mother's independence, and her father's tyranny in using his daughter as a marriageable commodity.

Providing a testimony which survives unmutilated is remarkable. Her tale of fleeing patriarchal oppression reaches the surface layer of such a complex novel, and is thus placed at the structural and thematic centre of the work. Safie becomes the active author of her own tale; her 'unmutilated' letters are read and reread many times, not only by Felix and Agatha De Lacey, but also by the creature, his creator and by Robert Walton. Walton confirms that he too only believes the tale of Victor Frankenstein through the existence of those letters. '[Frankenstein's] tale is connected,' he observes, 'and told with an appearance of the simplest truth; yet I own to you that the letters of Felix and Safie, which he shewed me [. . .] brought to me a greater conviction of the truth of his narrative than his asseverations, however earnest and connected.'[91] In stark contrast to the undamaged testimonies of Felix and Safie, Walton observes that Frankenstein 'corrected and augmented' the notes that he took, defending himself thus: 'I would not that a mutilated [narration] go down to posterity.'[92]

Gothic literature frequently concerns itself with the moments when manuscripts and letters are subject to partial translation, or become unreadable, effaced by time. Again, we can think here of the damaged, accidentally discovered manuscripts of Walpole's *The Castle of Otranto* and Ann Radcliffe's *The Italian*. Unreadable, poorly translated or partial manuscripts carry the risk of changing tales, effacing stories, silencing heroines who have been subject to enforced marriage, long-term imprisonment or even death. Manuscripts which are 'corrected and augmented', as Frankenstein does to the notes of Walton, increase the risk of silencing the victims. This is the fate not just of the creature, whose conversations with his creator are given more 'life and spirit', but also the destiny of the majority of female characters. Narrated through the lens of Frankenstein and Walton, we discover that Caroline Beaufort (later to become Frankenstein's mother), as a young woman confronted with family impoverishment, works for a living, plaiting straw, while tending her sick father. When her father dies, she is left 'an orphan and a beggar', who is only rescued by the 'protecting spirit' of her father's friend, who first takes care of her financially before marrying her two years later. There is, however, a contradiction in that story, for it is clear that she has cared for her father and provided financially for them both, but is curiously left 'an orphan *and* a beggar' on his death.

The death of Caroline from scarlet fever is recounted as sacrifice, for she catches it after tending Elizabeth Lavenza. Elizabeth is then implored by Caroline to 'supply my place to your younger cousins', and to marry Victor. Elizabeth's story is never fully told; she is only revealed very partially through the small nuggets of character that Victor chooses to reveal to us. The glimpses that we do gain of this orphaned cousin of Frankenstein are of a rational if superhumanly patient female character. Elizabeth swiftly supplants Caroline as the sacrificial victim there to service the needs of others' illnesses and afflictions, but never of sufficient significance to be protected fully. As Elizabeth dies at the hands of the vengeful creature, we learn only of her 'shrill and dreadful scream' from afar, whereas the effect of that scream on Victor is described in full anatomical detail. 'As I heard it,' he records, 'the whole truth rushed into my mind, my arms dropped, the motion of every muscle and fibre was suspended; I could feel the blood trickling in my veins, and tingling in the extremities of my limbs.'[93] Reduced, at last, through her dying scream to becoming merely one in a long chain of horror effects on Frankenstein, Elizabeth's story is never fully told. Her silence, as with Caroline's silence before her, says more about the narratological, Promethean obsessions of Frankenstein and Walton.

In contrast to the 'shrill and dreadful scream of Elizabeth', Safie's direct testimony is remarkable, a clear articulation of a proto-feminist message that pulses to the surface of this complexly structured novel while all other females are silenced through death. If Mrs Saville, that opening, silent addressee seems at first to conform to this pattern, then one must bear in mind her silent editorship of the entire text. At one point, one imagines that it is she who notes 'Walton, in continuation', a gesture that places her close to the authorship, readership and source of the novel, the real MWS. She *is* the eighteenth-century enlightened reader, but a reader who is conditioned, one imagines, to look with scepticism and foreboding on the tales of terror that her brother unfolds in his letters.[94]

In the later revised 1831 edition of the novel, Mary Shelley would sharpen the theme of understanding feeling that permeates the work. She did this by having Robert Walton confess to his sister, 'There is something at work in my soul that I do not understand.' That 'something at work' can be described as the Gothic in *Frankenstein*. So often viewed as being at odds with the Romantic project that mapped the ascendancy of the imagination, the Gothic in *Frankenstein* rests not so much in the physical presence of the nameless creature, but in the attempts to locate and anatomise the 'something at work in my soul' by articulating the inarticulate. Where that remains impossible, *Frankenstein* instead exposes what remains unspoken in the competing, often contradictory narratives of the novel. After Walton has recounted the full tale to his silent sister, he asks of her, 'do you not feel your blood congealed with horror, like that which even now curdles mine?'[95] Whereas Victor's blood tingles and trickles in his veins as he hears the scream of Elizabeth Lavenza, suggesting animation and excitement on his part, Walton, by contrast, anticipates that his sister's blood might cease to circulate, become suspended, at the horror of his tale. We never find out whether Mrs Saville's blood has 'congealed with horror', but the survival of the manuscript suggests that she has found remedy through the articulation of the story. It is our job, as enlightened readers of *Frankenstein*, placed as we are so closely with Margaret Walton Saville, to explore the impulses behind feelings and the contradictions that they produce in all of the characters who tell us their stories. Such is the Gothic quest of *Frankenstein*.

Successive generations of critics have pored over *Frankenstein*, taking from it what they wish. For some, it can be read as a metaphor of industrialisation, for others as a psychobiographical reading of Shelley's relationship with her parents and dead children; to others, as I have explored, it serves as a metaphor of the anxieties surrounding scientific research during the Romantic period. There is a danger attendant on these selective readings, however. Fred Botting, for one, has warned of this critical tendency to 'assemble [our] own monsters from the partial and dead signifiers that make up the narrative bodies of *Frankenstein*. Critics suture these fragments into their own commentary to produce new and hideous progenies that have lives of their own.'[96] Just as Victor Frankenstein concentrates on the parts rather than the whole of his creation, separating out the parts of the novel *Frankenstein* also risks ignoring the terrifying sublimity of the novel's entirety.

This is a novel that is above all about origins. *Frankenstein* scrutinises the origins of organic life, it traces the first impulses of human feelings in a bid both to acknowledge their force and regulate them, and it invites its readership to detect these origins through the palimpsestic layers that it accretes. At its heart, through that one comment 'Walton, in continuation', we detect the silent female. Combining the roles of author, editor and primary reader, the rational role of Margaret Walton Saville in *Frankenstein* lies at the structural and thematic core of the tale. Silent she may appear, but her independence of judgement pulses through the paratextual layers of the tale, in how she assembles them, and in how she clearly refuses to grant her brother Robert Walton the approval that he so craves. The authorship, testimony and rational judgement of the female heroine or victim are the most transformative measures that Mary Shelley brought to the Gothic genre with *Frankenstein.*Whilst she had taken much from the generic Gothic topoi of lost manuscripts, artistic heroines and charistmatic villains, it is her subtle transformation of the female character into the source of rational judgement and authorship that most resonates, and that endures into her later works as well.

Female testimony became something of a preoccupation for Mary Shelley, as she was forced to defend her authorship of *Frankenstein* from the very year in which it was published. Scott's review for *Blackwood's* echoed speculations about the authorship of the novel, commenting that it 'is said to be written by Percy Bysshe Shelley, who, if we are rightly informed, is son-in-law to Mr Godwin'.[97] Mary Shelley's reaction to this review was decisive. Writing to Scott from Bagni di Luca on 14 June 1818, she pointed out his error, noting that 'I am anxious to prevent your continuing in the mistake of supposing Mr Shelley guilty of a juvenile attempt of mine; to which – from its being written at an early age, I abstained from putting my name – and from respect to those persons from whom I bear it.'[98] Coyly modest and respectful of her family name at first glance, the rapidity of Mary Shelley's response to Scott's review is nonetheless decisive in its assertion of her authorship. In spite of this, and the numerous journal entries that she herself made where she noted her intense and lengthy work on the manuscript, it is surprising to note a tendency both in scholarship and fiction to challenge her sole authorship of the novel. Sadly, some authors have even gone so far as to argue that Percy Bysshe Shelley was in fact the sole author, owing in part to his extensive annotations of the manuscript. But here I agree with Daisy Hays, who argues that the alterations made by Percy Bysshe Shelley to the original manuscript are 'those of a sympathetic and careful reader, rather than of a man attempting to impose his intellectual philosophy on a woman's work', forms of collaboration that demonstrate 'Romantic sociability at its best: equitable, constructive, sympathetic and incisive'.[99]

Co-operation and editorial support characterised the working relationships of Mary and Percy Bysshe Shelley, and of Mary Shelley and Lord Byron. But her assertion of her own authorship to Scott in 1818 indicates an early anxiety about recognition, and about the relationship of what she wrote to both her husband and her father Godwin. Should an author actually intrude on their work in order to be recognised? The addition of the initials M.W. S. to *Frankenstein* suggests that Mary Shelley thought so. The value of authorial intrusion was an issue of confidence, difference and assertion that Mary Shelley was later to explore in 'Giovanni Villani', an essay that she published in *The Liberal* in 1823. 'Giovanni Villani' only tangentially touched on what she called 'the dear, rambling, old fashioned pages' of the sixteenth-century Florentine author who 'makes the persons of Dante's Spirits familiar to us'.[100] Villani was a familiar and oft-cited authority on Dante that Mary drew on frequently, but here she uses him in order to explore the 'frequent fault among modern authors, and peculiarly among those of the present day, to introduce themselves, their failings and opinions, into the midst of works dedicated to objects sufficiently removed, one might think, from the dangers of such an incursion'.[101] If this seems at first glance to be censorious of such authorial intrusions, it is not. Shelley goes on to argue that 'the glaring defects of the intrusion of self in a work of art' when 'well-managed', can 'excite stronger interest' than anything else, 'awaken[ing] a chord which else had slept'. This argument, articulated some five years after the first publication of *Frankenstein*, carries perhaps a note of regret that the authorial intrusion in *Frankenstein* had not been stronger. But that intrusion, as we shall see in the following chapter, was something that she pursued to even more extreme effect in her next work *Matilda.* So much more explicit and biographical was the female testimony in that work that it remained unpublished until 1959.

2

Testimonial and Refusal in Matilda *(1819)*

The earth was to me a magic lantern and I [a] gazer, and a listener, but no actor.

(*Mathilda,* chapter XII)

[U]ntil I knew Shelley I may just say that [Godwin] was my God – and I remember many childish instances of the excess of attachment I bore for him. This is past – all good is past for me, and all feelings except painful ones are far less vivid within me since life has become the solitude for me.

(Mary Shelley to Jane Williams, Genoa, 5 December 1822)

Mary Shelley wrote *Matilda* in 1819 at the age of twenty-two. It was around the time of the fifth anniversary of her elopement with Percy Shelley, an era that Emily Sunstein describes as 'the most extreme chiaroscuro period of her life'.[1] In September 1818 their daughter Clara had died from fever, and in June 1819 their beloved son William died of malaria and was buried in Rome. Mary began her novella only a month after William's death. At first it took the title *The Fields of Fancy*, a title that explicitly recalls Mary Wollstonecraft's 'Cave of Fancy', where the protagonist resists her passion for an unhappily married man. Whether, as Emily Sunstein speculates, Wollstonecraft's story particularly resonated with her daughter, who had not been able to resist her passion for an unhappily married man, is open to interpretation. What we can say is that *Matilda*'s eponymous heroine, like Mary Shelley herself, is motherless, and there are particular moments which map onto the author's experiences, as I will go on to explore.

Matilda was at first drafted as a dream narrative in the vein of Dante's *Divine Comedy*. Her journals in 1819 show how closely she was reading Dante's *Purgatorio* during the August of that year. Other notable reading in 1819 included *Oedipus* by Sophocles and Coleridge's drama *Remorse* (1813), a play that she had seen performed in London with her father in 1813. Her journal also notes that Percy was writing *The Cenci* during the August of 1819, the drama that, of all of his later writing, carried the most explicitly Gothic theme in its exploration of incest.[2] *The Fields of Fancy* gradually changed shape and title as Mary continued redrafting it in early 1820. From being a dream-narrative, it curiously became one of her works that ostensibly seems to be the most critical of dreaming as it probes the unintended consequences of dreams morphing into action.

When the finalised *Matilda* was sent to William Godwin in May 1820 in London for him to supervise its publication, he withheld its publication and refused to return the manuscript to Mary. He objected strongly to the incest theme, and found the subject 'disgusting' and 'detestable'.[3] The novella's portrayal of the excessive, incestuous attachment that subsists between the eponymous heroine and her father was bold, but not entirely new. Horace Walpole's *The Mysterious Mother* (1768), which told the tale of a mother who contrives to sleep with her son and conceives a daughter by him, had been published and freely available as part of his complete works since 1798; Mary was also translating Alfieri's *Myrrha* (1785), a tale of father–daughter incest based on Ovid's *Metamorphoses*; and Percy Shelley was also completing his drama of incest *The Cenci*.

The heroine's name brings to mind that of Walpole's Matilda in *The Castle of Otranto* (1764), who dies at the hand of her father's sword after having been too obedient and submissive to him throughout her life. Since Walpole's Matilda, the Gothic novel had treated of incest either covertly or explicitly in a range of works. There is the implied incestuous desire of the monk Schedoni in Ann Radcliffe's *The Italian* as he prepares to stab the heroine Ellena in the breast, but more explicitly in Lewis's *The Monk* (1796) there is the rape of Antonia by Ambrosio. The demon Matilda gleefully reveals to Ambrosio at the end of the novel the sibling connection between the monk and his victim Antonia. Sentimental treatments of incest, as Dale Townshend explains, were also in circulation at the time of Shelley's composition, but were decidedly different in tone:

> In its vivid articulation of the desires of the Gothic daughter, *Matilda* stands in stark relation to the exploration of father/daughter relationships in sentimental fictions the likes of Amelia Opie's *The Father and Daughter.* What distinguishes Shelley's novella so sharply from other fictional treatments of the father/daughter relationship of the period is her bold sense of the daughter as both the subject and object of desire.[4]

Whilst demonic female characters had been treated as the *subjects* of desire quite extensively in the Gothic (here, for example, we can consider Walpole's 'mysterious mother' who consciously and manipulatively sleeps with her son, Lewis's demoniac Matilda who seduces Ambrosio the Monk, Charlotte Dacre's Victoria di Loredani, who pursues the brother of her husband in *Zofloya, or the Moor* (1806) and Percy Shelley's own anti-heroine Matilda who murders for passion in *Zastrozzi*), the reciprocity of desire between father and daughter had not before featured so explicitly in Gothic novels.

This deviation from the models of previous Gothic fiction offers an insight, I think, into the radical message of *Matilda*. Mary Shelley herself acknowledged, as my second epigraph for this chapter indicates, an 'excessive attachment' that she entertained towards her father Godwin until the moment that Percy Bysshe Shelley entered her life. That clarity of insight also pervades this novella, as Matilda daydreams romantically about her absent father. But *Matilda* goes further than this too; it becomes just as much an exploration of how one acknowledges and then attempts to contain 'excessive attachment'. Like *Frankenstein*, *Matilda* also demonstrates that it is one thing to experience terror, horror, hatred, desire, but quite another to act on those feelings. The method of containing such extremes of feeling, and one which places *Matilda* close to *Frankenstein*, lies in the scope and extent of a humanitarian education. As I will argue in the remainder of this chapter, *Matilda* closely explores the experiencing, and then the containment, of extreme forms of feeling such as horror and terror. In the opening and final acts that make explicit reference to the heroine's suicide, we read something that is not a Gothic tale of terror, but rather a rational, if misguided, attempt to escape from the strength of imagination.

Written in the first person, addressed to her friend the poet Woodville, the narrative immediately draws attention to the solitary death of its author. 'I know that I am about to die and I feel happy – joyous,' Matilda confesses.[5] There is a blend of physiological and spiritual symptoms of approaching death recorded as Matilda observes, 'I feel my pulse; it beats fast: I place my thin hand on my cheek; it burns: there is a slight, quick spirit within me which is now emitting its last sparks.'[6] The Promethean underscoring of the spirit's 'last sparks' connects the tale with that of *Frankenstein,* but here, it is a heroine who takes the audacious decision to die. The tale is told as she dies, and takes the confessional form of an extended 'tragic history'.

We learn first of all in the narrative of Matilda's family history. This portion of the story focuses on the education of her father and mother as much as their characters. Her father was 'a man of rank', we learn, who had 'natural abilities' as a schoolboy, but 'discarded books' whilst at college, considering 'study as a school-boy shackle'.[7] 'He felt himself superior in quickness of judgement to those around him: his talents, rank and wealth made him the chief of his party, and in that station he rested not only contented but glorying, conceiving it to be the only ambition worthy for him to aim at in the world.'[8] The complacency of his superiority, education and ambitions, however, is explicitly condemned by his daughter, as she comments quite specifically on the 'strange narrowness of ideas' that he entertained.[9] Like Victor Frankenstein and Robert Walton in *Frankenstein,* he selects and discards his reading as he pleases. The difference with *Matilda,* however, resides in the explicit condemnation of those readings in the daughter's testimony. Matilda assumes the narrative judgement that is implicit but nonetheless absent from the epistolary *Frankenstein*. We learn of the father's reading from Matilda that 'Novels and all the various methods by which youth in civilized life are led to a knowledge of the existence of passions before they really feel them, had produced a strong effect on him who was so peculiarly susceptible of every impression.'[10] His susceptibility to every impression leads to a reckless lack of judgement, a premature indulgence in passion and an impulsiveness in his character that is barely checked.

Temporarily, we learn, the father is rescued from this by his early devotion to Diana, his childhood love. Diana's education has not been neglected, nor has she discarded it. Her father 'had devoted himself to the care of her education', focusing in particular on the 'heroes of Greece and Rome or with those of England who had lived some hundred years ago'.[11] Although this education is described as 'peculiar', it is not condemned. We learn that 'her knowledge was of a deeper kind and laid on firmer foundations' than that of Matilda's father. She is both a reincarnation of Elizabeth Lavenza, and possibly of Margaret Walton, as well as an anticipation of Shelley's next heroine, Euthanasia in *Valperga*. She is also invested with some of the qualities that Mary Shelley took from the works of her own mother, Mary Wollstonecraft. Diana is looked on by Matilda's father as 'a guide', providing the pedagogic and nurturing role to the father that he himself has fled early in his life. She thus becomes the active educator, curbing the passions of her husband. The tragedy, however, is that, like Mary Wollstonecraft, Diana dies only a few days after the birth of Matilda. The response of Matilda's father is predictably extreme: he is 'overpowered' by a fearful gloom, and quits the family home, abandoning his daughter.

Mary Shelley was not immediately abandoned by her father. On the contrary, in the wake of his wife's death, he agonised over the education of their two daughters Fanny and Mary, describing the dead Wollstonecraft in a letter to Amelia Anderson as 'the best qualified of any person I ever saw' to educate her children.[12] His premature remarriage to Mary Jane Clairmont, in his desperation to supply their daughters with a surrogate mother, caused friction with Mary who, as she exhibited her impatience and disdain of her new stepmother, was sent away for a long period of her adolescence to stay with the Baxter family near Dundee. The setting of Matilda's adolescence is clearly modelled on the youthful experiences of the author. Although Mary Shelley enjoyed staying with the Baxter family in Scotland, forming a strong friendship with their daughter Isabel, she also felt that she had been sent into exile. Matilda is a solitary individual who is reared on the shores of Loch Lomond by a distant Aunt who repulses all attempts at affection. The lack of parental affection and guidance that Matilda receives is explicitly condemned by her, in a vein that is similar to the complaints on self-education from Robert Walton and Victor Frankenstein. 'Almost from my infancy I was deprived of all the testimonies of affection which children generally receive,' complains Matilda; and 'I was thrown entirely on my own resources, and I enjoyed what I may almost call unnatural pleasures, for they were dreams and not realities.'[13] This observation is offered later in the narrative, after a substantial portion of the unhappy tale has been recounted by the heroine. It is in this later self-appraisal that Matilda is able to rehearse what she calls 'the different scenes of my short life', and to anatomise her dreams as 'unnatural pleasures'.

Prior to the self-awareness that accompanies the acknowledgement of her 'unnatural pleasures', however, Matilda describes her youthful dreams differently but no less disturbingly:

> I was a solitary being, and from my infant years, ever since my dear nurse left me, I had been a dreamer. I brought Rosalind and Miranda and the Lady of Comus to life to be my companions, or on my isle acted over their parts imagining myself to be in their situations. Then I wandered from the fancies of others and formed affections and intimacies with the aerial creations of my own brain – but still clinging to reality I gave a name to these conceptions and nursed them in the hope of realization [. . .] My favourite vision was that when I grew up I would leave my aunt, whose coldness lulled my conscience, and disguised like a boy I would seek my father through the world. My imagination hung on the scene of recognition; his miniature, which I should continually wear on my breast, would be the means and I imagined the moment to my mind a thousand and a thousand times, perpetually varying the circumstances. Sometimes it would be in a desart; in a populous city; at a ball; we should perhaps meet in a vessel; and his first words constantly were, 'My daughter, I love thee!'[14]

The miniature as a medium of recognition was a staple of Gothic fiction, arising in the plots of novels by Ann Radcliffe, Maria Regina Roche and many others. Matilda's ardent yearning for such a scenario suggests that, like her father, she has placed her faith too early in '[n]ovels and all the various methods by which youth in civilized life are led to a knowledge of the existence of passions before they really feel them'. While her aunt's library affords her some reading of the classics, including Shakespear [*sic*], Milton, Livy and Rollin, Matilda's haphazard reading of these classics bears more than a little affinity with that of the creature's haphazard classical reading in *Frankenstein*. The consequences are similar: she brings literary characters 'to life to be my companions', she confesses, 'or on my isle acted over their parts imagining myself to be in their situations'. Unlike the supervised education of her dead mother, Matilda's education has no guidance, no firm foundations. Without the crucial discernment that allows the separation of reality and dreaming, she herself begins to frame the parting letter from her father, at this stage the only writing of his that she has, in explicitly romantic terms. She rereads the letter constantly, and takes his words 'One day I may claim [Diana] at your hands' too literally. 'I was to be his consoler, his companion in after years,' Matilda resolves.[15]

Matilda describes the transformational nature of her father's return to her in post-lapsarian fashion. Whereas before, her 'life had been [. . .] as a pleasing country rill, never destined to leave its native fields', on his return 'it seemed to me as a various river flowing through a fertile and lovely landscape, ever changing and ever beautiful.'[16] No sooner is this Edenic metamorphosis noted, however, than its fall is observed in a way that anticipates her eventual suicide through poison: 'I drank of an enchanted cup but gall was at the bottom of its long drawn sweetness.'[17] Matilda's father is described by her as having 'the imagination of a poet' whose feelings are subject to 'a whirlwind'. An elderly servant in her father's home notes that her father spends the first night of their reunion in his home outside on the grass, groaning perpetually, and says, 'it wrings my heart to see my lord in this state.' E. J. Clery rightly observes the connections between Joanna Baillie's drama *De Monfort* and *Matilda* in these descriptions of the father's passions and the elderly servant's concerns about them. In Baillie's *De Monfort* it is the servant who first draws attention to his master's mental disorder, observing that 'he is much changed from what he was.' There is a clear verbal echo of this in *Matilda.* As it progresses further, Matilda observes that 'It was only when he was absent from me that his passion subdued him, – that he clinched his hands – knit his brows – and with haggard looks called for death to his despair, raving wildly, until exhausted he sank down nor was revived until I joined him.'[18] Matilda attempts to read her father's frenzy, asking, 'Could there be guilt in it?' and ascribes his 'tumultuous starts and gloomy looks wholly to the struggles of his mind and not any as they were partly due to the worst fiend of all – Remorse'.[19] Mary had read Coleridge's 1813 play *Remorse* in 1819, but she had also seen it performed, as Richard Holmes has noted in his biography of Coleridge, in 1813 at Drury Lane.[20] Coleridge depicted his two central protagonists Alvar and Ordonio as dreamers, observed Henry Crabb Robinson of his experience of the play. In *Matilda,* the father figure is also clearly depicted as a dreamer with the imagination of a poet. His disposition, however, places him closer to Coleridge's villain Ordonio than it does to his other more sentimentally driven character, Alvar.

Matilda, as I have argued, figures dreams negatively as 'unnatural pleasures'. As the heroine begins to observe her father's disorder, she starts to figure herself dangerously as the deliverer of her father, the damsel who can rescue him from his torture. When she seeks to discover her father's secret, he warns her that 'In the heart of one like me there are secret thoughts working, and secret tortures which you ought not to seek to discover.'[21] But like the Gothic heroine that she at this point views herself to be, she is intent on uncovering those 'secret tortures'. Her father's resistance is unavailing:

> He snatched his hand from me, and rose in violent disorder: 'What do you mean? You know not what you mean. Why do you bring me out, and torture me, and tempt me, and kill me – Much happier would [it] be for you and for me if in your frantic curiosity you tore my heart from my breast and tried to read its secrets in it as its life's blood was dropping from it. Thus you may console me by reducing me to nothing – but your words I cannot bear; soon they will make me mad, quite mad, and then I shall utter strange words, and you will

> believe them, and we shall be both lost for ever. I tell you I am on the verge of insanity; why, cruel girl, do you drive me on: you will repent and I shall die.'
>
> When I repeat his words I wonder at my pertinacious folly; I hardly know what feelings resistlessly impelled me. I believe it was that coming out with a determination not to be repulsed I went right forward to my object without well weighing his replies: I was led by passion and drew him with frantic heedlessness into the abyss that he so fearfully avoided – I replied to his terrific words: 'You fill me with affright it is true, dearest father, but you only confirm my resolution to put an end to this state of doubt.'[22]

If it is the father who raves, in the vein of a Gothic villain such as Baillie's tragic De Monfort, declaiming that he is 'on the very verge of insanity', then Matilda's resolution to discover his secret passion is described in similar vein as 'folly'. Her depiction of herself owes more than a little to Godwin's hero Caleb Williams, who, intent on discovering his employer Mr Falkland's guilty secret, also questions what drives him on in the wake of denial. Matilda cannot analyse 'what feelings resistlessly impelled' her.

Feelings, and the ability to acknowledge, understand and control those feelings, are, as I argued in my chapter on *Frankenstein*, a central preoccupation of Mary Shelley's fiction. *Matilda* clearly situates this inability to govern impulse in the haphazard education of the father and daughter who too swiftly position themselves as tragic characters. This applies as much to Matilda as it does to the father.[23] At one point, echoing Shakespeare's comedy *As You Like It*, Matilda confesses that 'Again and again I have passed over in my remembrance the different scenes of my short life: if the world is a stage and I merely an actor on it my part has been strange, and, alas! tragical.' That knowing performativity is grounded in Matilda's unchecked childish dreaming in Scotland, and her self-fashioning as heroines from Shakespeare and Milton. It goes beyond the realm of acting, and becomes a governing metaphor for how Matilda casts her life. Again, there is more than a little of Godwin's Caleb Williams in the disposition of Matilda. Caleb Williams opens his confessional tale by declaiming that 'My life has been a theatre of calamity,' and proceeds to narrate his tale in the vein of tragic hero.

Matilda's tendency to do the same is a troubling echo of a persecuted character.

Such knowing theatricality becomes all the more marked after the revelation of the father: 'My daughter, I love you!' where he goes on to compare himself to 'the fallen archangel' who has 'dashed from the top of the rock to the bottom!'[24] Matilda's response at first echoes her father's disorder:

> Yes it was despair I felt; for the first time that phantom seized me; the first and only time for it has never since left me – After the first moments of speechless agony I felt her fangs on my heart: I tore my hair; I raved aloud; at one moment in pity for his sufferings I would have clasped my father in my arms; and then starting back with horror I spurned him with my foot; I felt as if stung by a serpent, as if scourged by a whip of scorpions which drove me – Ah! Whither? Whither? [25]

Matilda again casts herself in the role of tragic heroine here, and offers to her reader a particularly visual embodiment of her grief, an embodiment that no doubt owed much to the acting that the young Mary Godwin had observed when she attended the performance of Coleridge's *Remorse.* There is a choreography of advance and retreat in her actions that mirrors the simultaneous attraction and repulsion that she feels towards her father.

Such physical embodiment of Matilda's remorse, however, seems to be cathartic, for immediately after this paroxysm of passion, she observes in a rather wry manner, 'Well, this could not last.'[26] At this point she disentangles her subjectivity from that of her father, and speaks of 'his unnatural suffering', reflecting that 'I gazed on him as to take my last farewell.' In the vein of a Gothic heroine who flees from physical assault, repulsion prevails as she secludes herself in her chamber 'in a retired part of the house' and indulges in 'better hopes for my future life' whilst consigning him to wandering for 'another sixteen years'. The separation of subject and object has begun, and persists as she hides herself in her room as she hears her father's footsteps pause outside her chamber in characteristically Gothic fashion.

For Matilda, the paroxysm of insanity is temporary; she is able to regain control of herself far more quickly than one might imagine.

Whilst her father should 'wander as an unlaid ghost and find no quiet from the burning hell that consumed his heart', she by contrast resolves that 'The mutual link of our destinies is broken.'[27] Her father's departure and suicide is recounted in tragic terms, with Matilda pursuing him with the elderly servant across England. But crucially, Matilda confesses that she feels no horror:

> I often said to myself, my father is dead. He loved me with a guilty passion, and stung by remorse and despair he killed himself. Why is it that I feel no horror? Are these circumstances not dreadful? Is it not enough that I shall never more meet the eyes of my beloved father; never more hear his voice; no caress, no look? All cold, and stiff, and dead! Alas! I am quite callous [. . .][28]

This is a reversal of the blood-curdling terror that Robert Walton wills his sister Margaret to experience in *Frankenstein*, of the horror that overwhelms Victor Frankenstein as he gazes on his nameless creation. Matilda experiences her lack of sensation as unfeeling, willing herself to experience the physical sensations of horror as some sort of moral duty. But the sought-for emotion never arrives.

Matilda fashions herself as a passive bystander of life, stating at one point that '[t]he earth was to me a magic lantern and I [a] gazer, and a listener, but no actor.' But her theatrical metaphors contradict this, suggesting conversely a strong sense of agency on her part. When she retreats to the seclusion of the Northumbrian countryside, she fashions herself in a nun's habit and acts the role of a penitent. It is in this guise that she befriends her fellow recluse Woodville, an ethereal poet in mourning after the death of his beloved, who subsequently becomes the addressee of her testimony. Clearly modelled on Percy Shelley, Woodville 'was glorious from his youth' and '[h]is heart was simple like a child, unstained by arrogance or vanity.'[29] In spite of his bereavement, Woodville cannot participate in the melancholia of Matilda. As she invites him to share the laudanum with which she intends to kill herself, Woodville refuses in the hope that 'in some way my labours may form a link in the chain of gold with which we ought all to strive to drag Happiness from where she sits enthroned above the clouds, now far beyond our reach.'[30] Although Woodville argues for civic duty as a reason in itself to remain alive, Matilda's counter-argument for death can also be argued as a rational choice. Matilda believes that her soul is 'corrupted to its core by a deadly cancer' and that 'if day after day' she 'dwelt on these dreadful sentiments', she would become insane. Her resolution to commit suicide, then, can be read as a reasoned response to the feared encroachment of horror. Reading Matilda's suicide in relation to David Hume's eighteenth-century essays which controversially defended suicide, 'Of Suicide' and 'Of the Immortality of the Soul' (1782), Michelle Faubert also supports the view that suicide is a rational and ennobling alternative in *Matilda*.[31] As Matilda records her slow rapprochement to death, she resolves of her father's death and the contemplation of his corpse that 'I will not continue to trace this frightful picture.'[32] Her female testimony reins in the imagination of her intended reader, Woodville. Reversing *Frankenstein*'s particularly masculine narrative exultation in the evocation of terror and horror, *Matilda* refuses to indulge in prurience and sensationalism by averting her addressee's gaze from her father's corpse and the grim and horrific details of her own death. Instead, we are left with an organic vision of growth: 'Farewell, Woodville, the turf will soon be green on my grave; and the violets will bloom on it.'[33]

The Gothic essence of *Matilda* lies not in any lurid depiction of incestuous desire, or indeed not even in the threat of incest. Instead, the female protagonist's testimony of her father's paroxysms of passion reveals both a refusal to succumb to the same internalised horror of her father and a restraint in her narration of the incestuous desires that both share. Mary Shelley's own admission of her worship of her father in the letter that she wrote to Jane Williams from Genoa in 1822 (cited in this chapter's epigraph) also demonstrated a similar restraint. After admitting her early strong feelings for her father, Mary then notes, 'This is past – all good is past for me,' firmly relegating her 'childish instances' of 'excessive attachment' to the past. *Matilda* too recognises the potency of the heroine's feelings for her father, but firmly relegates them to the 'childish' past. In the denial of a tale that can curdle the blood with horror, that can make the hair stand on end, there is a legitimate agency. Knowing when *not* to reveal the full extent of horror, of depravity, of desire, *Matilda* suggests, is a vital lesson that teaches us how to curb the excesses of our imaginations. As I shall argue in the following chapter, this is an insight that Mary Shelley carried forward to the depiction of her two heroines in *Valperga*.

3

Of Women, History and Romance in Valperga *(1823)*

> We look back to times past, and we mass them together, and say in such a year such and such events took place, such wars occupied that year, and during the next there was peace. Yet each year was then divided into weeks, days, minutes, and slow-moving seconds, during which there were human minds to note and distinguish them, as now. We think of a small motion of the dial as of an eternity; yet ages have past, and they are but hours; the present moment will soon be only a memory, an unseen atom in the night of by-gone time. A hundred years hence, and young and old we shall all be gathered to the dust, and I shall no longer feel the coil that is at work in my heart, or any longer struggle within the inextricable bonds of fate. I know this; but yet this moment, this point of time, during which the sun makes but one round amidst the many millions it has made, and the many millions it will make, this moment is all to me.
>
> (Mary Shelley, *Valperga*, p. 305)

Thus speaks Euthanasia, one of the two heroines of Mary Shelley's first historical novel *Valperga: or, the Life and Adventures of Castruccio, Prince of Lucca.* The idea of the novel was first conceived by Mary Shelley in 1817, worked on between the years of 1819 and 1821, and then published in 1823. From that temporal proximity to *Frankenstein* it is easy to trace shared concerns and themes. In the Preface to the novel, Shelley had recorded accurately her sources for the Life of Castruccio, detailing 'Machiavelli's romance concerning this chief', Sismondi's delightful publication, *Histoire des*

Républiques Italiennes de l'Âge Moyen as well as works by Tegrino and Giovanni Villani.'[1] A further historical source from the pen of Moreri, perhaps added in by Godwin, is also quoted at length in the Preface.[2] Combined, the laboured recording of these sources intentionally bear testament to an impressive weight of historical research on the life of Castruccio del Antelminelli. Such research did not go unremarked by reviews of the novel, which, as Mary Shelley anticipated, inevitably drew comparisons with *Frankenstein*, and marked the changes in tone approvingly. *The Ladies' Monthly Museum*, for example, observed that whereas 'In *Frankenstein* the author suffered imagination to riot unchecked amidst the regions of romance: in *Valperga*, the excursive faculty is restrained within moderate limits, and judgment asserts her legitimate authority.'[3] The reviewer for *The Examiner* also viewed the historical novel as a more legitimate form than the riotous romance genre, observing that while *Frankenstein* 'was doubtless extravagant', 'The publication before us being an historical novel, is free from this objection.'[4]

While the historical framework of *Valperga* diminishes the critical charges of 'extravagance' that accompanied the reception of *Frankenstein*, what critics overlooked was *Valperga*'s interrogation of the historical novel's ability to sustain the values of moderation and legitimacy. In the epigraph to this chapter, Euthanasia ventriloquises some of the major anxieties surrounding the Romantic period's relationship with history, and how the relationship between history and the individual ran the risk of occluding the individual's intimate relationship with 'the unseen atom' of 'the present moment'. As the Gothic romance had also charted again and again, this occlusion was most particularly striking in the relationship between women and history. Female authors such as Clara Reeve, Sophia Lee, Ann Radcliffe, Eliza Parsons, Eleanor Sleath, Maria Regina Roche, Jane Austen and Mary Shelley renegotiated the porous boundaries of romance, historical novel and 'Gothic Story' in order to explore the hidden, often Gothic histories of women, those dissonances between female experience and the more formal annals of history. Jane Austen's heroine Catherine Morland from *Northanger Abbey* (1818) states the case more bluntly but just as effectively as Shelley's later heroine Euthanasia when she complains to Henry and Eleanor Tilney that history "'tells me nothing that does not either vex or weary me. The quarrels of popes and kings, with wars or pestilences, in every page; the men all so good for nothing, and hardly any women at all – it is very tiresome.'"[5] Whereas wars, pestilence, quarrels and conquests can be recorded with relative ease, the passions and emotions of those who suffer the effects of war, such as Shelley's heroine Euthanasia, are lost to the annals of history. 'This moment is all to me,' Euthanasia observes in a profound moment of self-awareness as she contemplates the momentous transformation of her circumstances in the course of one day as Castruccio's army razes her castle to the ground.

While that moment may have been 'all' to Shelley's heroine Euthanasia, her experience of it (had she been based on a real character from history) would not have been recorded in the annals of history. While Shelley's Preface conscientiously records the historical and fictional sources that she has consulted in her construction of Castruccio, the end of the novel makes it clear that the composition of this history is derived from the private chronicles of Euthanasia. Euthanasia is an exceptional heroine: classically educated, humane and principled. The survival of her chronicle of Castruccio thematically places her close to her fictional predecessor Safie from *Frankenstein*, whose testimony of rebellion against patriarchal abuses of power also remains. They are both characters who hold revolutionary potential as they compose their tales, tales which survive the spoils of time and conflict. The narrative, describing Euthanasia's early education (where, like a Miltonic amanuensis, she reads to her blind father) focuses both on her affection towards her father, and the independence of her learning:

> A priest of a neighbouring chapel was her tutor; and the desire of pleasing her father made her indefatigable in her exertions. The first difficulties being conquered, she passed whole days over these dusky manuscripts, reading to the old man, who found double pleasure in the antient poets, as he heard their verses pronounced by his beloved Euthanasia. The effect of this education on her mind was advantageous and memorable; she did not acquire the narrow idea of the present times, as if they and the world were the same, which characterizes the unlearned; she saw and marked the revolutions that had been, and the present seemed to her only a point of rest, from which time was

> to renew his flight, scattering change as he went; and, if her voice or act could mingle aught of good in these changes, this it was to which her imagination most ardently aspired.[6]

Euthanasia's arduous programme of classical learning is noted approvingly quite specifically because it avoids promulgating a 'narrow idea of the present times, as if they and the world were the same'. Percy Bysshe Shelley's conception of classical learning and its value in interpreting the past is both inscribed and questioned here. In a letter that Percy Shelley is believed to have written 'To a Lady' in the Spring of 1821, he praised the 'sacred talisman of language', arguing that 'Facts are not what we want to know in poetry, in history, in the lives of individual men, in satire, or panegyric. They are the mere divisions, the arbitrary points on which we hang, and to which we refer those delicate and evanescent hues of mind, which language delights and instructs in precise proportion as it expresses.'[7] It is Euthanasia's communication and pronunciation of the 'antient' poets to her father that delights him, rather than the substance of what she communicates. Euthanasia's conception of the present moment further owes something to Percy Bysshe Shelley's conception of time in his famous 'Ode to the West Wind', which was composed in 1819 and published with *Prometheus Unbound* in 1820. The poet's incantation to the West Wind, the 'dirge / Of the dying year' which 'scatters' dead leaves, to 'Make me thy lyre' is an ode of desperate optimism about the future, an ode that sees within the seeds of the scattered leaves of the past the germination of the future. The position adopted by Euthanasia may be more modest, marked by conditionals and hesitation – 'the present *seemed* to her only a point of rest, from which time was to renew his flight, scattering change as he went; and, *if* her voice or act *could* mingle aught of good in these changes, this it was to which her imagination most ardently aspired' (my emphases) – but the crucial element is that this conception of past, present and future is dynamic, and one in which Euthanasia as a woman aspires to be an active agent. It is a conception of time in which the imagination is the key factor.

The Gothic's dynamic engagement with versions of history throughout the eighteenth century sought to fictionally excavate the private chronicles of individual characters who otherwise disappeared from the grand, political histories of the age. Conjectural history, as Mark Salber Phillips has observed, was not a 'political narrative' but 'a moral science held together by the desire to investigate the fundamental principles of human nature'.[8] Shelley's *Valperga* participates in that investigation. For here, as Sonia Hofkosh has insightfully argued, a consideration of the 'representation of history' transforms into a study of 'the history of representation'.[9] Shelley's study of the 'history of representation' was informed simultaneously by her fascination with reading histories, and her fascination with reading Gothic tales. She appreciated that the two modes of writing were, of course, not mutually exclusive. The cross-pollination of Gothic romance and history took place largely in the eighteenth century. Prévost d'Exiles, a French author, is widely recognised for introducing into England a particular brand of historical romance in the 1730s through his historical romance *Clèveland*, which retold historical events through the eyes of an imagined illegitimate son of Cromwell.[10] Through this focus, Cromwell emerges as even more cruel, ambitious and tyrannical than histories had portrayed him.[11] Baculard d'Arnaud further capitalised on the possibilities offered by Prévost's extensive historical romance, retelling or reinventing (among others) in his *Histoires Anglaises* the story of the pretender to the English throne Perkin Warbeck. Both *Clèveland* and *Warbeck* were later reinterpreted by Sophia Lee through her historical Gothic romances *The Recess* (1783–5) and *Warbeck: A Pathetic Tale* (1786). Tilottama Rajan has noted how Mary Shelley's *Valperga* shares a similar aim to Lee's *The Recess* in its recovery of 'a lost female genealogy'.[12] *The Recess* had adapted Prévost's *Clèveland,* and constructed a tale about two imagined daughters of Mary, Queen of Scots, Matilda and Eleanor, who are hidden away from the vindictive and paranoiac investigations of Queen Elizabeth I. In composing tales about female characters, real or imagined, who were materially affected by the civil wars and machinations that constituted the chronicles of history, both Sophia Lee and Mary Shelley could challenge what Margaret Anne Doody in her analysis of women's Gothic authorship memorably called the 'falsehood and disorder' of the 'real world'.[13]

In the wake of such private chronicles of history as those offered by Prévost, d'Arnaud and Sophia Lee, William Godwin lent his critical voice to the growing chorus of authors who broached the thorny, fragile relationship between romance and history in his 1797 essay 'Of History and Romance'.[14] There, discussing Prévost's use of historical licence, Godwin commented on the comparative shortcomings of history. To his mind, history veered uneasily between providing a 'mere skeleton' of facts and offering 'conjectures' respecting the motivations of its objects of study. Romance, by contrast, and more specifically, historical romance (as practised by Prévost among others) was the superior form of writing in its ability to 'analyse the materials of which [society] is composed':

> Laying aside the generalities of historical abstraction, we must mark the operation of human passions; must observe the empire of motives whether grovelling or elevated; and must note the influence that one human being exercises over another, and the ascendancy of the daring and the wise over the vulgar multitude. It is thus, and thus only, that we shall be enabled to add, to the knowledge of the past, a sagacity that can penetrate into the depths of futurity [. . .]
>
> The writer of romance is to be considered as the writer of real history; while he who was formerly called the historian, must be contented to step down into the place of his rival, with this disadvantage, that he is a romance writer, without the arduous, the enthusiastic and the sublime licence of imagination, that belong to that species of composition. True history consists in a delineation of consistent, human character, in a display of the manner in which such a character acts under successive circumstances, in showing how character increases and assimilates new substances to its own, and how it decays, together with the catastrophe into which by its own gravity it naturally declines. [15]

Godwin here demonstrates his preference for individual stories, stories that are able to demonstrate and articulate the 'successive circumstances' and complex motivations of the individual in order to look more effectively at 'the depths of futurity'. This type of scrutiny, he argues, cannot be achieved in the types of mass history that populate circulating libraries in multiple volumes; for Godwin, instead, these types of historical examinations are to be found in the genre of historical romance. Godwin warns that 'The reader will be miserably deluded if, while he reads history, he suffers himself to imagine that he is reading facts.'[16]

Godwin's defence of the superior values of historical romance derived, in part, from a broader revalorisation of the uses of romance that was propounded by Bishop Richard Hurd in his *Letters on Chivalry and Romance* (1762) and, later, by Clara Reeve, in her defence entitled *The Progress of Romance* (1785). There, Reeve had noted of the romance that 'The learned men of our own country, have in general affected a contempt for this kind of writing, and looked on Romances, as proper furniture only for a lady's library.'[17] One might be forgiven, too, for thinking that William Godwin himself was sceptical about the values of romance, when his first novel, published in 1794, *Things as They Are, or the Adventures of Caleb Williams*, displayed its tragic hero Caleb and his adversary Falkland as dangerously in thrall to tales of romance, adventure and chivalry. The scepticism about romance that *Caleb Williams* seems at first glance to display, however, is qualified on closer scrutiny. It is not so much the consumption of tales of adventure, chivalry and romance *per se* that Godwin questions, but the monomaniacal consumption of them by Caleb and Falkland. Godwin is concerned more by questions of excessive and uncritical reading, concerns that also later lurk at the margins of Austen's *Northanger Abbey*. Godwin uses verbs such as 'devour' and 'imbibe' to describe his characters' fascination with chivalry and romance in *Caleb Williams*, illustrating that those characters have an unhealthy and undiscriminating appetite for those tales. Discrimination, for William Godwin, was crucial to the engagement with historical romance as a viable alternative to the drier annals of history. In 'Of History and Romance', Godwin embellishes his privileging of romance with a pseudo-scientific language, arguing that romance could better display the organic 'decay' and 'decline' of character under a chain of circumstances. Romance's delineation of character here assumes the mantle of investigative logic, and becomes the better instrument through which to analyse how 'catastrophe' affects an individual.

This is precisely the strategy that Mary Shelley adopts in *Valperga*, where her character from history, Castruccio, is shown to 'decay' and 'decline' under his unflagging pursuit of conquest, revenge and war. As I noted earlier, we discover that it is Euthanasia who describes the decay and decline of Castruccio, her childhood friend, and later her betrothed. Historical accounts of Castruccio, such as that of Machiavelli's *Life of Castruccio*, refer to him as a 'great Hero' whose 'Graces increased with his Years'. [18] Such histories, however, exclude the type of forensic examination of motivation, decay and ambition that Godwin had advocated, and that Mary Shelley offers to us in *Valperga*.

The subtitle of the novel, *The Life and Adventures of Castruccio, Prince of Lucca*, lend the novel a resonance of the eighteenth-century picaresque novel, such as Laurence Sterne's 1759 *The Life and Opinions of Tristram Shandy, Gentleman.*[19] At first, the narrative follows the picaresque tradition with the adventures of Castruccio being told in considerable detail from when he leaves the familial home at the age of fourteen. Castruccio is at first awarded a fine interior consciousness, demonstrated for example in the episode when, as a young man, he happens on a re-enactment of Dante's *Inferno* on the River Arno:

> The infernal drama was acted to the life; and the terrible effect of such a scene was enhanced, by the circumstance of its being no more than an actual representation of what then existed in the imagination of the spectators, endued with the vivid colours of a faith inconceivable in these lethargic days.
>
> Castruccio felt a chill of horror run through his frame; the scene before him appeared for a moment as a reality, rather than a representation; the Arno seemed a yawning gulph, where the earth had opened to display the mysteries of an infernal world; when suddenly a tremendous crash stamped with tenfold horror the terrific mockery.[20]

Shelley displays her ever-evolving fascination with terror, horror and effect here, as she explores with forensic detail the terror that derives from an 'actual representation of what then existed in the imagination of the spectators'. It is a meta-commentary on performativity, on the re-enactment of passion and emotion, and of how that re-enactment can create the emotion of horror within the minds and hearts of its audience. Castruccio, we learn, 'felt a chill of horror run through his frame' as the scene appears 'as a reality, rather than a representation'. If at first this passage seems far removed from the confines of the historical novel, it is because it *is*. It concerns the superior powers of representation and imagination over reality and, more specifically, the reality 'of these lethargic days'. Casting a critical nod towards the present times, Castruccio's 'chill of horror' at the 'yawning gulph' of the inferno cannot, Shelley argues, now be experienced because of our comparative lack of intensity when it comes to matters of faith. The episode seems for a moment almost nostalgic for this strength of feeling, but it swiftly undercuts this nostalgia by the merging of reality and representation. There is a 'tremendous crash' as the bridge of Carraia collapses – an event that actually took place in 1304 and that was vividly recorded by Giovanni Villani's *Chronicles* – and Castruccio, standing at a distance, is helpless in the face of the catastrophe:[21]

> The bridge of Carraia, on which a countless multitude stood, one above the other, looking on the river, fell. Castruccio saw its props loosening, and the curved arch shake, and with a sudden shriek he stretched out his arms, as if he could save those who stood on it. It fell in with a report that was reverberated from the houses that lined the Arno; and even, to the hills which close the valley, it rebellowed along the sky, accompanied by fearful screams, and voices that called on the names of those whom they were never more to behold. The confusion was beyond descriptions terrible; some flying, others pressing towards the banks of the river to help the sufferers; all, as himself, seized with a superstitious dread, which rebuked them for having mimicked the dreadful mysteries of their religion, and which burst forth in clamorous exclamations and wild horror. The heroism of Castruccio failed; he seized with eagerness the opportunity of an opening in the crowd; and, getting into a by street, ran with what speed he could, while his knees still shook beneath him, from the spot he in the morning as eagerly sought.[22]

Castruccio's reaction in the face of physical catastrophe is to freeze, to be rendered helpless in the wake of real catastrophe. It is a reaction that was recorded frequently by theorists and practitioners of Gothic terror alike. John and Anna Laetitia Aikin's 'On the Pleasure Derived from Objects of Terror' (1773) had explored how the experience of terror, whether through reading or spectating, could force us through 'actual torture – through the relation of a Damien's execution, or an inquisitor's act of faith'.[23] In Charles Robert Maturin's 1820 novel *Melmoth the Wanderer*, too, the character Monçada, an unwilling novice monk, observes at one remove his helplessness when watching a crowd execution, the 'horrid trance' that suspends him, and compels him to witness the scene of cruelty. He observes that 'The drama of terror has the irresistible power of converting its audience into its victims.'[24] Such a realisation haunts Shelley's Castruccio, who still at a young and impressionable age, yet retains the capacity for self-reflection and self-chastisement at this point in the narrative: '"If I had been on that bridge," – he could no longer resist his emotions; tears ran fast down his cheeks, and he sobbed aloud.' Mary Shelley, as E. J. Clery observes in *Women's Gothic*, was 'a diligent student of [Joanna] Baillie's work, and may well have been led to it by her father's call to lay aside "the generalities of historical abstraction" and "mark the operation of the human passions".'[25] Baillie's 'Introductory Discourse' to her first volume of *Plays on the Passions*, seen as an important precursor of William Wordsworth's later Preface to *Lyrical Ballads*, insisted on the examination of individuals in intimate and domestic moments in order better to chart the progress of their passions. Baillie's aim was consonant with what Godwin had argued for in his unpublished 'Of History and Romance' and with Shelley's later aims in *Valperga*. During the picaresque episodes that Shelley imagines from Castruccio's younger life, we see our historical hero weeping, acting impetuously, finding himself unable to act and judging the other characters he encounters with degrees of severity.

As the narrative of the life and adventures of Castruccio unfolds, however, the interior life of Castruccio slowly diminishes, and our capacity to appreciate what Godwin had called in 'Of History and Romance' 'the operation of the human passions' in Castruccio is increasingly limited. *Valperga* awards an increasingly theatrical tone to the actions and aspirations of Castruccio, noting, for example, that he 'dreamed of futurity; and the uncertainty of his destiny only gave more scope to his imagination, as he figured the glorious part which he flattered himself he was about to act on the great theatre.'[26]

The 'glorious part' which he is about to play, however, involves successive conquests – of women, territories and properties. He becomes the Promethean overreacher, like his predecessor Victor Frankenstein, who only figures futurity in terms of acquisition. Castruccio's dreams of futurity here form part of what Joseph W. Lew has noted as a 'dark portrait of Imagination' that illustrates the links between 'male Romantic ideology and the growth of the empire'.[27] In direct proportion to the monstrous growth of Castruccio's ambitious imagination, however, the narrative interest in the interior life of Castruccio diminishes. His role in the 'great theatre' of life is described in increasingly performative terms. He becomes an actor, skilful in his preparation, who 'had studied human nature with the observant eye of genius; and all careless as he appeared to be, he had learned how to please the multitude, how to flatter the foibles of the noble, and thus to gain the hearts of men and to rule them.'[28] The mediation of Castruccio's studied posturing suggests that as he develops the aptitude to perform acts of flattery, so too does he lose some of his own essence. His manipulation, flattery and praise of others become increasingly reminiscent of other literary characters:

> Castruccio was fond of power; yet he was neither arrogant nor tyrannical; words of kindness and winning smiles he bestowed at will on all around. He appeared to fit himself for each scene in which he was to take a part; in the camp he was energetic, valorous, and swift of action; in council he was as prudent and cautious as a grey-haired minister of state: at balls, or during a hunting-party, he recommended himself by grace, agility, wit, and a courtesy whose sweetness was untarnished by vanity or presumption. His beauty took a more manly cast; and somewhat of pride, and more of self-confidence, and much of sensibility, were seen in his upturned lip; his eyes, dark as a raven's wing, were full of fire and imagination; his open forehead was shaded by the hyacinthine curls of his chestnut-coloured hair. His face expressed extreme frankness, a frankness that did not exist in his mind; for his practices among the wily chiefs of Lombardy had robbed him of all ingenuousness of soul, although the traces of that which he once possessed had not faded from his countenance.[29]

As Castruccio rejects the valued counsel of retirement advocated by his mentor and family friend Guinigi, his tutelage at the hands of the brutal warrior Alberto Scotto in France, and of the demonically acquisitive Benedetto of Cremona, takes its toll; he modulates his actions according to whom he speaks with, fitting himself 'for each scene in which he is to take a part' to the extent that even his outstanding beauty is tellingly described as a 'cast'. Neither his ambition nor his beauty are original, but are moulded instead from the 'cast' of others. This is a reference, perhaps, to Mary Shelley's extensive, sophisticated and clever use of literary allusion. There is more than a little of Milton's Satan in these descriptions of Castruccio; the references to the traces of ingenuousness in Castruccio's 'countenance' being 'not yet faded' at the end of this particular passage recall the careful balance that Satan maintains between the cruelty of his eye and his casting of 'signs of remorse' as he manipulates those around him in Book I of *Paradise Lost*:

> [H]e, above the rest
> In shape and gesture proudly eminent,
> Stood like a Tower; his form had yet not lost
> All her original brightness, nor appeared
> Less than Archangel ruined, and th'excess
> Of Glory obscured: as when the Sun new ris'n
> Looks through the Horizontal misty Air
> Shorn of his Beams, or from behind the Moon
> In dim Eclipse disastrous twilight sheds
> On half the Nations, and with fear of change
> Perplexes Monarchs. Darkened so, yet shone
> Above them all th'Archangel: but his face
> Deep scars of thunder had intrenched, and care
> Sat on his faded cheek, but under brows
> Of dauntless courage, and considerate pride
> Waiting revenge: cruel his eye, but cast
> Signs of remorse and passion to behold
> The fellows of his crime [. . .][30]

In this particular description of Satan, Milton's choice of extended elemental similes of the sun looking 'through the Horizontal misty

Air' and the Moon 'in dim eclipse' underscores the *process* of glory fading, a 'form' that '*had yet not lost / All her original brightness*' (my emphases). Shelley's description of Castruccio similarly partakes of that process, with the 'traces' of former glory and ingenuousness not yet 'faded'. The consequences of these allusions are to emphasise the gradual, organic, tragic loss of those qualities in Castruccio, and to suggest the importance of external influences in the loss of those qualities. His association with the 'wily chiefs of Lombardy', his chance encounter with the Machiavellian Benedetto of Cremona (Pepi) and consorting with ruthless warriors have all left their marks. Betrothed to Castruccio, Euthanasia's 'penetrating judgement' soon discerns the character of her lover:

> He was formed for victory and daring, rather than for magnanimity; he was swift of design and steady in execution; bold, valiant, yet gentle of manner; his wit was keen; his penetration into the dispositions of men instantaneous; and he possessed also, as by instinct, the faculty of adapting himself to every character, and of acquiring the love of all around him: men always love those who lead them successfully through danger. He was temperate in his habits; and in his mien, though the exterior were ardent and even rash, there might be perceived underneath a reserve of caution, a presence of mind, which never permitted him to be carried beyond the dictates of prudence, and an eagle-eye which caused him swiftly to distinguish danger from impracticability. He trod the most perilous activities, but his foot was sure like that of the chamois; and he would discern from afar where the path was broken, and would check himself in the most headlong course. All this was well, but, underneath a frankness of nature, there was the craft of a grey-haired courtier, and even at times the cruelty of a falling tyrant. Euthanasia saw not all this; but at times a glance, a tone seemed to open a mine of undiscovered evil in his character, that made her shudder in the very depths of her nature: yet this sensation would pass away, and she, prompt to forget evil in others, thought no more of it.[31]

Euthanasia discerns the balance of Castruccio's good qualities of leadership, courage and prudence with his capacity to become 'a falling tyrant', but the narrative makes it clear that she 'saw not all of' his potential for evil. Her own love of wisdom and liberty fosters a comparative innocence; 'prompt to forget evil in others', Euthanasia wrongly dismisses her instinctual fears of Castruccio's tyranny. The classic Gothic romances by Radcliffe and Lewis in the 1790s taught a heroine either to obey her instincts, or else to endure the consequences. We can think here of Emily St Aubert in Ann Radcliffe's *The Mysteries of Udolpho* carefully reading and taking heed from the countenance of the villain Montoni; and the converse in Lewis's victimised heroine Antonia, who listens to a gypsy's song at the end of chapter 1 of *The Monk* that predicts her grisly fate at the hands of a seducer, is troubled by the warning, but then promptly forgets about it. The gypsy's prophecy is grimly fulfilled to full effect towards the close of *The Monk*, suggesting that we ignore warnings at our peril. Shelley's Euthanasia, owner in her own right of the castle of Valperga where 'alone among the wild Appenines she studied and worshipped nature', 'pored over the works she had before read with her father' and nurtured 'the creative fire in her heart and brain', partakes of the many excellent qualities of the Radcliffean Gothic heroine in her worship of sublime beauty, her study of the classics and her enjoyment of solitude. One could argue, however, that although Euthanasia is perfectly able to read the signs of evil in the character of Castruccio, her inability or unwillingness to act on them is what determines her fate, and the loss of her castle.

The fact that Mary Shelley changed the title of her novel to *Valperga*, the name of Euthanasia's cherished castle that Castruccio destroys, highlights the Gothic significance of that castle. Working in the vein of Horace Walpole and Ann Radcliffe, who both named Gothic romances after castles (*The Castle of Otranto* (1764), *The Mysteries of Udolpho* (1794) respectively), the reader is conditioned to view Valperga as the major site of contestation in the novel. Like Radcliffe, Shelley has an orphaned heroine who is the legal owner of the castle. *Valperga*, however, reverses the Radcliffean Gothic convention of the orphaned heroine first enduring adversity but eventually laying claim to the castle. At the beginning of the novel, Euthanasia is already in possession of her castle, but she loses it because she does not heed her judgement's instincts about the flaws in Castruccio's character. Castruccio and his men are not interested in staking a claim to Euthanasia's castle; in this regard, he is no

Gothic usurper like Walpole's Manfred or Radcliffe's Montoni. Castruccio instead lays claim to the castle in order to erase its existence. In this lies a crucial distinction in Shelley's revolutionary engagement with the modes of Gothic, history and romance. Castruccio's erasure of Euthanasia's castle is an attempt to erase her significance. He acts on the erroneous assumption that Valperga means everything to Euthanasia. His quest to sustain the supremacy of necessity includes the silencing of any counter-narrative, any voice of protest. Destroying Valperga is Castruccio's attempt to silence Euthanasia. Erasing her castle, Castruccio presumes, implies erasing all dissent for ever.

Castruccio's conquest of *Valperga*'s second heroine assumes a different complexion. Beatrice is first presented to us through the focalisation of Castruccio. Described at first through visual impressions, her description may seem familiar to any reader conversant with earlier examples of Gothic romance:

> In the corner of the vast apartment in which the assembly sat, were two women. One was old, and dressed in the fashion of an age gone by: she was in black as a widow; her vest was close and strait, trimmed with beads, and made of black cloth; a black veil covered her head, and her capuchin thrown aside discovered the years and wrinkles of the venerable wearer. It was impossible to judge of the age, and hardly of the sex, of the figure that sat beside her; for her capuchin was wrapped closely round her form, and the hood drawn over her face, as she sat silently, turned away from the company, in the darkest part of the room.[32]

Lewis's *The Monk* (1796) and Radcliffe's *The Italian* (1797) had both begun with a similar scene portraying two women, one old and one young, focalised through a male gaze.[33] Beatrice's introduction in *Valperga* is particularly similar to that of Lewis's tragic heroine/victim Antonia. Both have their features obscured by a veil and a capuchin hood, and, if anything, Beatrice appears to be more at pains to conceal her identity and her sex, wrapping the capuchin 'closely' around her body, and turning away from the company. The visual markers of Lewis's earlier Gothic romance are strikingly clear, but Shelley weaves subtle yet noticeable distinctions into her portrayal of Beatrice of Ferrara. While this opening description of her establishes the narratological cues for reading her as the sexual victim of Castruccio and others, the development of Beatrice's character, physiognomy and ability also separate her from the one-dimensional cipher of heroinism that Lewis's Antonia was. To begin with, it is the old lady, and not a young man or the movements of a faceless crowd, who reveals the face of Beatrice:

> As she spoke, she threw back the hood of her young companion, and Castruccio gazed on her exquisite and almost divine beauty. Her deep black eyes, half concealed by their heavy lids, her curved lips, and face formed in a perfect oval, the rising colour that glowed in her cheeks which, though her complexion was pure and delicate, were tinged by the suns of Italy, formed a picture such as Guido has since imagined, when he painted a Virgin or an Ariadne, or which he copied from the life when he painted the unfortunate Beatrice Cenci. Her jet hair fell in waving luxuriance on her neck and shoulders below her waist; and a small silver plate was bound by a white riband on her forehead. Castruccio could only gaze for a moment on this lovely being; for, turning a supplicating look on her aged friend, she again drew the hood over her face, speaking in so low a tone, that he could not distinguish the words she uttered;[34]

Again like Lewis's Antonia who, through the focalisation of Lorenzo, is compared with the Venus de' Medici, the beauty of Beatrice is framed by artistic simile. There are, however, several key differences in the portrayal of Beatrice, for here Shelley's narrator qualifies the 'divine beauty' of Beatrice with the word 'almost', and emphasises that the comparison of the beauty of Beatrice to the portraits of the Madonna and Ariadne by Guido Reni are resemblances that the artist has '*since* imagined' (my emphasis). What these qualifiers add to an otherwise overworked version of the Gothic fallen heroine is significant, for Mary Shelley's Beatrice has no original. Neither tragic heroine (Lewis's Antonia) nor female devil (Lewis's Matilda), Beatrice retains her agency as an independent, strong female at this point in the novel. If her agency is temporarily suspended by her older female guardian removing the capuchin from her, then she herself regains it by concealing herself again. We learn that Beatrice is the offspring of an extraordinary woman, Wilhelmina of Bohemia, who herself is arrested for blasphemy, and dies in the hands of the Inquisition. As Barbara Jane O'Sullivan explains, Shelley transcribes two passages from Muratori's *Antichrista Italiane* No. 60 which detail the heresy of Wilhelmina of Bohemia who believed that she was the Holy Ghost incarnate on Earth. To each passage that Shelley transcribed, however, she adds 'in favour of the female sex'.[35] The silencing and suppression of Wilhelmina, who dies punished in the Inquisition because of her female cult, suggests, as O'Sullivan notes, 'the existence of a conspiracy which suppresses the alternative visions of women and destroys their network'.[36]

Beatrice, the prophetess of Ferrara, and offspring of such an extraordinary woman has, as Barbara Jane O'Sullivan observes, an 'extraordinary character, whose very talents alienate her from the society in which she lives'.[37] As she is arrested and placed in the Inquisition for her prophecies, she shows no fear or repentance: she was 'all loveliness, all softness' the narrator notes, 'yet there was a spirit within her, which elevated her above, although it mingled with the feminine delicacy of her mind and manners.'[38] Yet again, a careful balance is maintained between femininity and agency, rendering Beatrice at once exceptional and normal. It is the latter quality that proves to be her downfall. As she is tried by the Inquisition for her prophecies, Castruccio 'would have darted forward to save her, but someone held him back.' She saves herself by passing over the burning shares with a quick light step, an act of exceptionalism that, to the partial eyes of Castruccio, renders her 'as inspired, as ethereal, but more lovely'.[39] It is her exceptionalism that draws Castruccio to her, an exceptionalism that also guarantees her eventual fall. As she too falls in love with Castruccio, Shelley's narrator switches tense to the present, and reinscribes the conventions of romance in, one is tempted to think, a world-weary tone:

> And does the beauteous prophetess seek her tower to behold the glories of the morn? Beatrice is on the *donjon* of the palace; and it is true that her eyes are directed towards the rising sun; but there is a casque which flashes under its first beams, a horseman who gallops away from Ferrara, whose form her eyes strain to behold, even when

> he appears only as a black spot in the distance. She leans her cheek on her hand, and, lost in meditation, she, most unfortunate, mistakes for the inspirations of Heaven the wild reveries of youth and love: but still her heart was hidden even from herself by a veil she did not even wish to throw aside.[40]

The narrative registers in the transition of tense a reliance on the conventions of romance. While Beatrice's eyes seek 'the rising sun', looking towards things of a more divine nature, the 'horseman who gallops away from Ferrara' eclipses her heavenly vision. The knight on the charger, so familiar a convention of medieval romance, is the agent that curbs Beatrice's independence and agency. Beatrice begins to feel mortal love, but in so doing, 'She felt her soul, as it were, fade away,' a feeling which the narrator clearly laments with the observation that 'these were her dreams, – alas! to her they were realities.'[41] There is a subtle condemnation, perhaps, of the overwhelming strength of her imagination, a condemnation that echoes *Frankenstein*'s condemnation of the Promethean overreacher.

As Beatrice casts off her diadem, so too she casts off her exceptional qualities, inviting Castruccio to meet her at the secret entrance of the viscountess's palace at midnight. The narrative makes an explicit connection between Beatrice's fall and the fall of a castle here. Castruccio, it observes, 'sought the secret entrance of the viscountess's palace', and was received by the beautiful Beatrice, enshrined in an atmosphere of love and joy.'[42] The repeated naming of the place of seduction – the viscountess's palace – sharpens the explicit connection that is being forged between the fall of Euthanasia's castle, Valperga, and the fall of Beatrice. The narrator compassionates Beatrice and laments her inheritance of 'the most ardent imagination that ever animated a human soul' from that of her mother. Her sexual fall from grace is not what is condemned here, but the 'mysteriousness and delusive sanctity' with which she invests her passion for Castruccio. He is invested with divine qualities by Beatrice. When, inevitably, he falls short of these expectations, admitting to a pre-existing preference for Euthanasia, she is undone because of the strength of her affection. Beatrice is discarded by Castruccio in the same way that he quickly and decisively dispenses with the castle of Euthanasia. Disposed of, she becomes a wanderer who falls prey to a particularly vile warrior Tripalda. He subjects Beatrice, we are led to understand, to a long imprisonment and repeated rape. By the time of her escape, she is haunted, hunted and prey to every form of villainy.

If the story of Beatrice seems relentlessly grim and pessimistic about the fate of exceptional women, there is yet one glimmer of hope that somewhat redeems the experience. This lies in the way that Beatrice will only offer an edited version of her misfortunes to Euthanasia, refusing to 'tell that which would chill your warm blood with horror'.[43] Beatrice may be ruined by her sexual contact with men, she may well be the Gothic victim that Lewis's Antonia also was, but unlike the explicit intentions of the narrative of *Frankenstein*, which is to 'chill your warm blood with horror', Beatrice withholds the salacious particulars of her degradation, curbing the horrors of her addressee Euthanasia, the reader and of herself. Horror, the aesthetic that both Burke, and Radcliffe later, had claimed as a negative affect, froze the imagination and suspended the actions of its recipient. This is what Castruccio experienced on the Bridge of Carraia in Florence, when the performance of Dante's *Inferno* turns into real horror and catastrophe. His actions are suspended, and he is unable to move. Beatrice, by contrast, consciously avoids arousing horror in her auditor, allowing the development of a more organic relationship between herself and Euthanasia.

It is Euthanasia, the other love interest of Castruccio, and the one who is able to 'give the reins to [her] feelings' who rescues and compassionates Beatrice. The two-heroine model that Shelley successfully adapted from the model of Sophia Lee's *The Recess* is not simply a passively recycled version; instead, Shelley places the emphasis on love, compassion and female companionship. Although Euthanasia in the end cannot save Beatrice, it is *their* relationship that is most vividly and warmly painted within the confines of this historical novel. Whilst drawing quite clearly on some of the tropes with which Matthew Lewis invested his Gothic victim Antonia in *The Monk*, Mary Shelley also reframes the fall of her heroine Beatrice. She is a woman of ardent imagination, one who actively solicits and negotiates the attentions of Castruccio, and one who survives those sexual encounters and subsequent more brutal ones at the hands of Tripalda in order to enjoy a warm and mutually beneficial relationship with Euthanasia. Whereas Matilda and Elinor, the two heroines of Lee's *The Recess* end up distanced, divided by the rivalry that exists between the men that they love, Euthanasia and Beatrice by contrast are united by the suffering that they have endured at the hands of Castruccio.

The revolutionary model of friendship that Shelley proposed between Beatrice and Euthanasia can be found elsewhere in her fiction: the relationship between Elizabeth Lavenza and Justine Moritz in *Frankenstein*, while narrated in less detail, also provides a model of a mutually sustaining friendship, invested with belief and strong feeling as Elizabeth visits Justine in prison. The forging of these benevolent, female friendships, Shelley argues, can serve to expunge, if only temporarily, the horrors to which the characters are otherwise exposed. In the end, Euthanasia cannot save Beatrice from the clutches of the charlatan witch Mandragola, who alongside the albino jester Bindo, can at first glance be read as particularly Gothic characters. At first, Beatrice allows herself to be seduced with the promises of being reunited with Castruccio by the charlatan witch Mandragola, (whose charlatanism is detailed quite explicitly by the narrator, thus deflating any sense of Gothic sublimity that she may otherwise arouse). It is, however, the absence and not the presence of Euthanasia that prompts Beatrice's actions, actions which ultimately lead to her death.

By the end of the novel, Castruccio has become an empty cipher of tyranny, brutality and heartlessness. All notions of chivalry, honour and glory have disappeared, and the narrator notes that 'he was hated by most, and feared by all.'[44] Like Shelley's earlier monster and creator, he is compared frequently with Milton's Satan, but it is the passages of *Paradise Lost* that trace the process of Satan's loss of glory that are echoed. '[T]hose passions whose outward signs he suppressed, yet preyed on the vital principle; his eyes had not lost their fire, but their softness was gone.'[45] The parasitical passions of ambition and revenge consume the flesh of his other, better qualities, leaving the host empty, with just a few barely palpable traces of former glory and chivalry.

Mary Shelley refines and reimagines Gothic convention in her development of both the hero and two heroines in *Valperga*. Just as Castruccio goes beyond the aspirations of the usurping Gothic villain in quest of the castle, so too Euthanasia exceeds the confines of the Gothic heroine's concerns with property and inheritance. Although Euthanasia laments the loss of her Valperga, this is not the end of her story. What matters most, instead, is Euthanasia's ability to offer solace and compassion to Beatrice, and to record their tales, stories that would otherwise remain hidden and untold.

As she imagined the destruction of Valperga, Shelley perhaps had in mind her mother Mary Wollstonecraft's rebuke in *A Vindication of the Rights of Men* (1790) of Edmund Burke's image of the desecrated castle when describing the destruction of constitution in his *Reflections on the Revolution in France* (1790):

> Why was it a duty to repair an ancient castle, built in barbarous ages, of Gothic materials? Why were the legislators obliged to rake amongst heterogeneous ruins; to rebuild old walls, whose foundations could scarcely be explored, when a simple structure might be raised on the foundation of experience, the only valuable inheritance our forefathers could bequeath?[46]

Wollstonecraft here recast the constitution of England as a decaying castle that should be razed to the ground rather than renovated. In so doing, she also challenged the rights of absolute monarchy. Euthanasia, as Joseph W. Lew notes, is furthermore named from Essay 7 of David Hume's *Essays, Moral and Political*, which Mary Shelley had read in December, 1817. There Hume had portrayed the terror of 'absolute monarchy' as 'the easiest death, the true *Euthanasia* of the British constitution'.[47] Euthanasia may be more sentimentally attached to her own castle Valperga than Wollstonecraft's earlier unsentimental account, but Wollstonecraft's emphasis on 'the foundation of experience' as 'the only valuable inheritance' is nonetheless important. Inheriting or appropriating property, bodies and material possessions is one thing, a particularly Gothic prospect, but in *Valperga* the survival of Euthanasia's testimony, the tale of two uncelebrated women, provides the 'foundation of experience' that challenges that Gothic narrative. Beatrice refuses to award space to the particular terrors to which Tripalda subjects her for three years as she tells her story to Euthanasia; in turn, Euthanasia refuses to augment and exaggerate the powers that Castruccio exercises over her by destroying her castle. Such alternative testimonies diminish the terrors evoked by absolutist figures like Castruccio. In a subtle rewriting and reprivileging of Gothic conventions, *Valperga* limits the potential that history holds to curdle our blood with horror as we contemplate the exploits of Castruccio. The Gothic past remains in the realm of imagination as we consume and apprehend it through the measured testimony of Euthanasia.

4

'On Ghosts' and The Last Man*: Mourning, Melancholia and Transformational Terror*

> This indeed was the plague. I raised his rigid limbs, I marked the distortion of his face, and the stony eyes lost to perception. As I was thus occupied, chill horror congealed my blood, making my flesh quiver and my hair to stand on end.
>
> (Mary Shelley, *The Last Man* (1826), ed. Anne McWhir, p. 203)

It was a mere eight years after the elopement of Mary Godwin and Percy Bysshe Shelley that the latter drowned with Edward Williams in the Gulf of Spezia on 8 July 1822. Fearing the worst after Shelley and Williams had set off on the ill-fated sailing excursion in the boat *Don Juan*, Mary had arrived at Byron's palace in Pisa around midnight, pale, distraught and still unwell after a recent miscarriage. Her appearance and conduct prompted Byron to reflect that he had 'seen nothing on the stage so powerful, or so affecting'.[1]

Grief is overwhelming; unrepresentable in its immediacy, and unbearable to the onlooker. 'Mary Shelley was in extremis,' Emily W. Sunstein remarks, since the premature death of Shelley left her 'incredulous, fearful, remorseful for what' was 'left unsaid and undone'.[2] The early unutterable stage of that grief is captured in a letter that Mary Shelley wrote to Thomas Medwin that was acquired by the New York Library in 2011 for the Carl H. Pforzheimer Collection.[3] Writing from Albaro, Genoa on 10 May 1823, Mary expressed her gratitude to Byron for his faithful continued attendance to her, and to Trelawny for his assistance in discharging the practical duties after Shelley's cremation. In the middle of her letter, she makes a direct reference to her state, speaking of 'the misfortunes that have come so thick on me and driven me to a state of utter hopelessness that all the world seems but a shifting sand beneath me'.[4] The final part quoted here is the only attempt at metaphor in the letter; Mary then stops herself, stating that she will complain no more. Sparse and controlled, this remarkable letter nevertheless offers a nascent articulation of a grief with which Mary Shelley would wrestle for many decades to come.

The key to beginning to articulate this intense grief came in March 1824 in the form of a short essay that Mary composed and published in the *London Magazine* entitled 'On Ghosts'. The piece begins by lamenting the passing of the 'antediluvian world, strode over by mammoths, preyed on by the megatherion, and peopled by the offspring of the Sons of God'. In our world of 'hedged-in corn-fields and measured hills', an age characterised by the explorations of Mungo Park, where the only land to be discovered is 'the interior of New Holland', the only uncharted sea (source of fascination and ambition to Frankenstein's Robert Walton) is the 'North West Passage', Mary Shelley asks 'What have we left to dream about?'[5] As she muses on this, she repeatedly asks 'Yet is it true that we do not believe in ghosts?'[6] The question becomes almost a plea, one that is answered by the Gothic. 'But let it be twelve at night in a lone house,' she advises; 'take up, I beseech you, the story of the Bleeding Nun; or of the Statue, to which the bridegroom gave the wedding ring, and she came in the dead of night to claim him, tall, white and cold [. . .] and let all these details be assisted by solitude, flapping curtains, rushing wind, a long and dusky passage, an half open door' and then 'another answer may be given.'[7] Of most significance are the time, atmosphere and circumstances in which one reads Matthew Lewis's 'The Bleeding Nun' from *The Monk,* for example. It is not the tale itself, Shelley argues, which will lead us to believe in ghosts, but the space in which we read that tale, the time of night at which we consume it.

Having established these accordant circumstances, Mary Shelley next begins the authorial intrusion that she had advocated only the year before in her essay 'Giovanni Villani' for *The Liberal.* There, as I charted at the end of Chapter 1, she had argued that a judicious assertion of the authorial self in a composition was at times desirable. 'To sit down for the purpose of talking of oneself, will sometimes freeze the warmth of inspiration,' she argued; 'but, when elevated and carried away by the subject in hand, some similitude or contrast may awaken a chord which else had slept.'[8] The repeated questions about belief in ghosts that she muses on in 'On Ghosts', the method by which she becomes excited about the 'flapping curtains, rushing wind, long and dusky passage': combined, these questions and Gothic effects transport her to the point where she at last feels comfortable in inserting her own experiences into the essay. And thus begins a tentative exploration of her grief, founded not on the image of the lost friend, but on the atmosphere in which she was able to evoke his ghost. It is a remarkably moving passage that deserves to be quoted at length:

> Some years ago I lost a friend, and a few months afterwards visited the house where I had last seen him. It was deserted, and though in the midst of a city, its vast halls and spacious apartments occasioned the same sense of loneliness as if it had been situated on an uninhabited heath. I walked through the vacant chambers by twilight, and none save I awakened the echoes of their pavement. The far mountains (visible from the upper windows) had lost their tinge of sunset; the tranquil atmosphere grew leaden coloured as the golden stars appeared in the firmament; no wind ruffled the shrunk-up river which crawled lazily through the deepest channel of its wide and empty bed; the chimes of the Ave Maria had ceased, and the bell hung moveless in the open belfry: beauty invested a reposing world, and awe was inspired by beauty only. I walked through the rooms filled with sensations of the most poignant grief. He had been there; his living frame had been caged by those walls, his breath had mingled with that atmosphere, his step had been on those stones, I thought: – the earth is a tomb, the gaudy sky a vault, we but walking corpses. The wind rising in the east rushed through the open casements, making them shake; – methought, I heard, I felt – I know not what – but I trembled.[9]

Solitude and twilight are two of the preconditions that Shelley established earlier in her essay for experiencing the supernatural, but here, in spite of the conducive atmosphere, she experiences difficulty in reviving the ghost of the beloved. This is a passage that thrives on negation; the pausing of the chimes of the Ave Maria, the 'moveless' bell and 'no wind' cannot assist in recalling the ghost of her friend.[10] But experiencing this absence by walking through the 'vacant chambers by twilight', Mary at last begins to feel something through the morbid transformation of the house which he inhabited, imagining his 'living frame' 'caged by those walls'. Only at that moment, when she makes the imaginative leap towards metaphorising that grief, when the earth becomes 'a tomb, the gaudy sky a vault, we but walking corpses' do the accordant circumstances of wind rushing through casements fall into place.

The process of grief was the task of the remainder of her life, but one which she began to confront through 'On Ghosts' and her novel of environmental catastrophe, *The Last Man* (1826). The elegiac, autobiographical nature of *The Last Man* is well known, but for the purposes of clarity I will rehearse it briefly. Percy Bysshe Shelley is reincarnated in the novel as Adrian, Earl of Windsor, who would have been destined for the throne had England not become a republic (in the course of the novel) in the year 2073, while Mary Shelley divides her own characteristics between two siblings: Lionel, the narrator of the novel, who marries Adrian's sister Idris, and Lionel's sister Perdita. Perdita marries Lord Raymond. Raymond was modelled on Lord Byron who died in Greece in the early months of the novel's composition. In the wake of Raymond's infidelity with a Greek princess called Evadne and his eventual death, Perdita commits suicide. Lionel, however, survives as the last man on earth.

Survival or suicide: in the wake of such intense and extensive loss in her life, it is hard to tell which of the two fates Mary Shelley would have preferred for herself, but in the recently discovered letter that I quoted at the beginning of this chapter, she tells Medwin how much she anticipates and looks forward to her own death. Mary's journals further reveal the extent of her desolation. On 14 May 1824 she alluded to the theme of her new novel in her journal: 'The last man! Yes I may well describe that solitary being's feelings, feeling myself as the last relic of a beloved race, my companions extinct before me.' She linked these emotions to a contingent 'failure of [her] intellectual powers' conceiving of her mind as 'a blank – a gulph filled with formless mist'.[11] *The Last Man* was the novel that temporarily filled that void. Its cathartic qualities become clear in the Introduction: 'My labours have cheered long hours of solitude,' she wrote, 'and taken me out of a world, which has averted its once benignant face from me, to one glowing with imagination and power.'[12] She refers to the depression and pain that the materials caused her, but reflects that 'such is human nature, that the excitement of mind was dear to me, and that the imagination, painter of tempest and earthquake, or worse, the stormy and ruin-fraught passions of man, softened my real sorrows and endless regrets.'[13] Exercising her imagination was the mode through which she chose to alleviate grief. But in that qualification of 'or worse, the stormy and ruin-fraught passions of man', we can see the grain of what matters most in *The Last Man*. The 'ruin-fraught passions of man', imaged through the real ruined buildings through which the last man on earth wanders, are a more urgent quest of Mary's exploration than the signs of environmental catastrophe.

The Last Man becomes progressively couched in the language of the Gothic as the plague takes hold of the global population. It charts the progressive growth of 'dread' within the human mind as it gains control over almost every character within the novel. In the epigraph to this chapter, our first-person narrator and the last man, Lionel Verney, examines the corpse of a man who has died from the plague. The confirmation of Lionel's worst fear, that 'this indeed was the plague', leads to a physiological reaction that is couched in almost precisely the same language of horror that Victor Frankenstein uses to describe his reaction to his creature, and that Robert Walton uses to his sister Margaret Walton Saville in *Frankenstein*: 'chill horror congealed my blood, making my flesh quiver and my hair to stand on end.' As it apprehends and digests the processes of personal grief that are inscribed in the intensely autobiographical aspect of the novel, so too does it tell us much about how to experience horror, and then move beyond it. *The Last Man* offers a particularly transformational and dynamic version of the Gothic, in showing its readership and its author the cathartic characteristics of horror and dread.

The topic that Mary chose for the first novel that she had written in the wake of the deaths of not only Shelley, but also Lord Byron and three of her children, was not new. Byron's poem 'Darkness', composed between 21 July and 25 August 1816, had already imagined environmental catastrophe in the wake of the eruption of Mount Tambora and 'the year without a summer'. Thomas Campbell's poem 'The Last Man' followed suit, although Campbell was later to argue that he had in fact been the originator of the theme.[14] Byron's 'Darkness' is framed in the terms of a dream, but the first line immediately qualifies this by saying that it 'was not all a dream'. The poem was an important context for Mary Shelley's later novel, for it charts, I think, something that is absolutely essential to *The Last Man* in the following lines:

> I had a dream, which was not all a dream.
> The bright sun was extinguished, and the stars
> Did wander darkling in the external space,
> Rayless, and pathless, and the icy earth
> Swung blind and blackening in the moonless air;
> Morn came and went – and came, and brought no day,
> And men forgot their passions in the dread
> Of this their desolation; and all hearts
> Were chilled into a selfish prayer for light:
> And they did live by watchfires – and the thrones,
> The palaces of crowned kings – the huts,
> The habitations of things which dwell,
> Were burnt for beacons; cities were consumed,
> And men were gathered round their blazing homes
> To look once more into each other's face;[15]

'Rayless', 'pathless' and 'moonless': as with Shelley's later essay 'On Ghosts', Byron begins with an accretion of negatives, but here they serve to emphasise the unfathomable actions of nature in the wake of environmental catastrophe. But as cities and homes fall prey to nature's altered behaviour, so too does the conduct of men transform. '[M]en forgot their passions in the dread / Of this their desolation.' The ascendancy of dread and terror over the everyday passions of men is something that Mary Shelley would also take up in *The Last Man*. Composed during intense and sustained bereavement, Shelley turned, as Gillen d'Arcy Wood observes, to describing a devastating plague that was based on 'descriptions of cholera coming out of India' and the 'morbid tallies of its victims'.[16] Moving from the personal loss of immediate friends and family to a 'post-apocalyptic description of a world depopulated by epidemic disease, with a tiny rump human community meditating on the end of history' may well appear, as d'Arcy Wood argues, 'more existential than romantic in character'. However, as I shall argue in the remainder of this chapter, as the apocalyptic tale evolves, so too do the characters' reactions to the epidemic. It is the framing of their reactions to death, rather than their quest for survival, that becomes the propulsion of the story.

'What a sea is the tide of passion,' Raymond reflects, 'whose fountains are in our own nature! Our virtues are the quick-sands, which shew themselves at calm and low water; but let the waves arise and the winds buffet them, and the poor devil whose hope was in their durability, finds them sink under him.'[17] Virtues, Raymond argues, are fickle characteristics that sadly are all too easily washed away by tides of passion. We can compare this back to Mary's only metaphor in her letter to Medwin, quoted at the beginning of this chapter, when she observes 'the misfortunes that have come so thick on me and driven me to a state of utter hopelessness that all the world seems but a shifting sand beneath me.'[18] Shifting sand, quicksands: the metaphors of erosion indicating the usurpation of moral certainty in both author and character are striking. They tell us of the transience of happiness, and of the equally important role that feeling plays in either diminishing or enlarging the calamitous events in our imagination. It is Raymond, described by Lionel as having a varied 'physiognomy' where 'every trait spoke predominate self-will,' who, subject to the waves and the winds of passion, is responsible for spreading the plague into England as he pursues his mistress Evadne to Greece. By turns 'unbending yet haughty, gentle yet fierce, tender and again neglectful', Raymond cannot master the contradictory, impulsive nature of his passions. He leaves behind his duties to England and his idyllic family life with Perdita. Impulsive action, the novel warns, can lead to the most devastating consequences, severing familial ties and compromising civic duty. This theme is echoed in the novel's epigraph, which is taken, like the epigraph to *Frankenstein*, from book XI of Milton's *Paradise Lost*: 'Let no man seek / Henceforth to be foretold what shall befall / Him or his children.'[19]

The Last Man is a novel of two parts. In the first, a pastoral setting around the Lake District and the Forest of Windsor enables Shelley to explore characters who are prey to their passions, but who also transform and regulate those selfsame passions. The narrator Lionel Verney, for example, first describes himself in Chapter 1 as 'an unprotected orphan among the valleys and fells of Cumberland'.[20] Narrating in retrospect, Lionel both wishes to evoke the reader's sympathy and draw attention to the self-pity that drove his early life. As a youth, he describes himself as one who is prey to 'gust[s] of passion'. Like Mary's earlier anti-hero Castruccio, the characteristics with which Lionel endows himself are reminiscent of the trammelled, confused emotions of Milton's Satan: 'I was angry, impatient, miserable,' observes Lionel; 'my only happy hours were those during which I devised schemes of revenge.'[21] His particular animus is directed against the son of the former King of England whose sovereign father Lionel suspects of having ruined his own father. At first glance, in the opening two chapters of the novel, this too, like *Matilda*, seems to be a tale preoccupied with fathers and their influences. As Perdita, Lionel's sister, dares to admire the young Earl of Windsor and hopes to meet him, Lionel spits out a speech that is worthy of Milton's Satan:

> His rank his least merit, do you say? Why, all his virtues are derived from his station only; because he is rich, he is called generous; because he is powerful; brave; because he is well served, he is affable. Let them call him so, let all England believe him to be thus – we know him – he is our enemy – our penurious, dastardly, arrogant enemy; if he were gifted with one particle of the virtues you call his, he would do justly by us, if it were only to shew, that if he must strike, it should not be a fallen foe. His father injured my father – his father, unassailable on his throne, dared despise him who only stooped beneath himself, when he designed to associate with the royal ingrate. We, descendants of one and the other, must be enemies also. He shall find that I can feel my injuries; he shall learn to dread my revenge![22]

Satan's fixation with vengeance against God in *Paradise Lost* is imbued with republican feeling against absolute authority. Here

Lionel also attempts to make this excuse to hate a prince that he has not yet met, calling himself, as Satan also does, 'a fallen foe'. Milton's development of Satan's contradictory feelings and enslavement to passion is also freighted into this early portrayal of Lionel. For as Satan agonises in *Paradise Lost*, 'Which way I fly is hell, Myself am Hell', so too does Lionel appreciate the war of passions within himself, that his hatred of others is also the 'last and worst degradation, to hate myself'.[23] Writing in retrospect, Lionel is able to appreciate the absolute danger that lurks within his character. In an image that is reminiscent of Byron's conflicted and doomed character Manfred standing in splendid isolation in the Alps while he reflects that 'though I wore the form / I had no sympathy with breathing flesh.'[24] Lionel observes of his imperilled situation:

> Thus I stood on a pinnacle, a sea of evil rolled at my feet; I was about to precipitate myself into it, and rush like a torrent over all obstructions to the object of my wishes – when a stranger influence came over the current of my fortunes, and changed their boisterous course to what was in comparison like the gentle meanderings of a meadow-encircling streamlet.[25]

Juxtaposing the torrent of bitterness and hatred which tempts him with 'the meadow-encircling streamlet' which at last vanquishes his internal struggle, Lionel invokes the pastoral mode that becomes so important to this section of *The Last Man*. Adrian, the Shelleyan figure, 'a tall, slim, fair boy, with a physiognomy expressive of the excess of sensibility and refinement', wins Lionel over. Looking on his 'beaming countenance', Lionel experiences an epiphany. This is his moment of spiritual conversion, where the 'gust of passion' yields to 'innocence and love' and his 'plastic soul [is] remoulded by a master hand.'[26]

Such descriptions of mastering the passions in a mode of spiritual conversion are important to *The Last Man* because they inscribe a fundamental distinction in this novel. As Mary had resorted to the annals of her history in *Valperga* to explore in Castruccio the development of another orphaned figure, she described an eventual fall, a gradual descent of her central male protagonist into a Satanic figure. Here, in this novel, set in the future in 2073 where England is already a republic, there is a reversal. Lionel begins as an orphan who obsesses about revenge and is prey to his passions, hating and suspecting all of those around him. But he is then converted to a safer stream of conduct, and is able to expel the 'gust of passion' from his character. Whereas Castruccio is contaminated by contact with his peers such as Alberto Scotto, Lionel is redeemed by the community that gathers around him. There is thus both much similarity and distinction between Castruccio and Lionel. Lionel is figured as the hero of continuity. He is the character who survives to tell his tale, since he has governed his passions. He navigates the apocalyptic catastrophe of the plague through his interaction with different versions of Romanticism. The Shelleyan idealism of Adrian, always described in ethereal, impermanent terms, leads to a weakness in his constitution, which makes him temporarily mad. It is up to Lionel to rescue Adrian from madness. Lionel also resists the blandishments of the Byronic conflicts of passion that shake Raymond, understanding that 'ambition' is the primary passion that motivates his friend. Such moral and intellectual lessons help him to withstand the plague. They are lessons which enable him to govern what is, as I will next argue, a particularly Gothic imagination. When the plague arrives, Lionel at first can only imagine its horrendous consequences in particularly morbid and lurid terms, but as he becomes more instrumental in the fight against it, so too does he learn to distinguish between his imagination and reality, thus curbing, taming and acknowledging his worst imaginings.

The pastoral, Edenic scenes of community and love between Lionel and Idris, Raymond and Perdita, with Adrian as their steadfast friend, take place in the Forest of Windsor. Mary and Percy had rented a brick cottage there with a flower garden during what was, according to Sunstein, 'the first relatively serene period of their union'.[27] That space is reimagined through the depiction of Perdita's cottage in the Forest:

> in her pleasant alcove, redolent with sweetest flowers, adorned by magnificent casts, antique vases, and copies of the finest pictures of Raphael, Correggio, and Claude, painted by herself, I fancied myself in a fairy retreat untainted by and inaccessible to the noisy contentions of politicians and the frivolous pursuits of fashion.[28]

Just as Elizabeth Lavenza copies paintings in *Frankenstein* for her pleasure rather than from competitive instinct, so too we learn that Perdita paints and copies for herself and her space. Although Morton D. Paley reads this copying as a symptom that Perdita 'finds no constructive outlet for her powers', if we read her characterisation in relation to Elizabeth Lavenza, we can discern a parallel in their dispositions and creative outlook.[29] Like Elizabeth, she too acknowledges the distinction between representing other paintings for one's pleasure, and 'emulating' others. A figuration of Mary Shelley, Perdita is independent, capable of finding pleasure in her own companionship, and of indulging in dreams for the sake of pleasure alone. Her space is, however, a utopian, idealised space, free as it is from the contaminations of the metropolis and politics. Her marriage to the more volatile Raymond compromises this utopian space, leading, as Raymond observes, to 'bitter and unreasonable imaginings'. Significantly, the destruction of Perdita's peace is heralded by the intrusion of Evadne, who previously rejected the suit of Adrian. Raymond rediscovers her living in poverty in London, designing a building for an architecture competition. Evadne executes her art with an aim, that being to rescue her from poverty. Although in this she is partially successful, her art does not make her happy, as she is more vulnerable to the 'gusts of passion' than Perdita.

Too soon, the plague arrives to destroy the utopian community that Lionel, Idris, Perdita, Raymond and Adrian have established in the Forest of Windsor. Rather than focusing in too lurid detail on its victims, Lionel first focuses on the spaces that have been inhabited by others. As in 'On Ghosts', space offers an important configuration of its inhabitants, opening up the potential for grief. As Lionel wanders towards Perdita's deserted cottage in the wake of the plague taking hold, he muses on the past, present and future:

> The trees moved overhead, awakening nature's favourite melody – but the melancholy appearance of the choaked paths, and weed-grown flower-beds, dimmed even this gay summer scene. The time when in proud and happy security we assembled at this cottage, was gone – soon the present hours would join those past, and shadows of future ones rose dark and menacing from the womb of time, their cradle and their bier. For the first time in my life I envied the

> sleep of the dead, and thought with pleasure of one's bed under the sod, where grief and fear have no power. I passed through the gap of the broken paling – I felt, while I disdained, the choaking tears – I rushed into the depths of the forest. O death and change, rulers of our life, where are ye, that I may grapple with you! What was there in our tranquillity, that excited your envy – in our happiness, that ye should destroy it?[30]

This meditation comes in the immediate wake of the plague's outbreak, and as Lionel meditates on futurity, all that he can now envision is the past as the utopian space, while the 'shadows of future' hours only rise 'dark and menacing'. It is worth noting that here Lionel is unable to bring himself to enter Perdita's cottage. Whereas in 'On Ghosts', the key to mourning lay in wandering through the house formerly inhabited by her friend, Lionel's premature attempt to come to terms with loss only leads to a bitter contemplation of futurity. He contemplates suicide, imagining with 'pleasure' a space 'where grief and fear had no power'. His vision is clouded by Gothic auguries of the future, leaving him unable to contemplate and manage the present.

Whereas in *Valperga*, as Castruccio destroys her castle, Euthanasia states that 'this moment is all to me,' Lionel by contrast cannot live in the moment. This emotional paralysis becomes even more explicit in his attendance at Alfred's birthday party. Morbidity clouds over the celebrations as Lionel begins to imagine his friends and family in some form of danse macabre:

> Ye are all going to die, I thought; already your tomb is built up around you. Awhile, because you are gifted with agility and strength, you fancy that you live: but frail is the 'bower of flesh' that encaskets life; dissoluble the silver cord that binds you to it. The joyous soul, charioted from pleasure to pleasure by the graceful mechanism of well-formed limbs, will suddenly feel the axle-tree give way, and spring and wheel dissolve in dust. Not one of you, O! fated crowd, can escape – not one! Not my own ones! Not my Idris and her babes! Horror and misery! Already the gay dance vanished, the green sward was strewn with corpses, the blue air above became fetid with deathly exhalations. Shriek, ye clarions! Ye loud trumpets, howl! Pile dirge on

> dirge; rouse the funereal chords; let the air ring with dire wailing; let wild discord rush on the wings of the wind! Already I hear it, while guardian angels, attendant on humanity, their task achieved, hasten away, and their departure is announced by melancholy strains; faces all unseemly with weeping, countenances thronged around, exhibiting every variety of wretchedness – well known faces mingled with the distorted creations of fancy. Ashy pale, Raymond and Perdita sat apart, looking on with sad smiles. Adrian's countenance flitted across, tainted by death – Idris, with eyes languidly closed and livid lips, was about to slide into the wild grave. The confusion grew – their looks of sorrow changed to mockery; they nodded their heads in time to the music, whose clang became maddening. [31]

Lionel's funereal imagination contorts what should be a celebration into his own personal vision of hell. Writing in retrospect, he is prescient enough to acknowledge that these are the 'distorted creations of fancy'. The morbid extent of his imaginative transportation is indicated by the passage's move into apostrophe. At first, Lionel internally addresses the birthday celebrants, saying 'Not one of you, O! fated crowd, can escape,' but as he becomes progressively engrossed in his vision, he begins to apostrophise the funereal instruments, exhorting the clarions to play, and the dire wailing to commence. As the passage slips into the form of an ode, so too does it contort those features, celebrating and commemorating only a warped image of futurity. Lionel's morbidity occludes reality; he sees his own wife Idris with 'livid lips' sliding into a 'wild grave'; the crowd becomes an assemblage of corpses who mock his living form.

Dread, horror and morbidity paralyse Lionel as his family falls prey to the effects of the plague. 'I longed to avoid the necessity of action,' he confesses; 'I strove to escape from thought – vainly – futurity, like a dark image in a phantasmagoria, came nearer and more near, till it clasped the whole earth in its shadow.'[32] We know from her journals that Mary Shelley had attended Professor Garnerin's lectures on 'Gas, Electricity, Aerostation, Phantasmagoria &c.' in December 1814, so she was conversant with the optical, and often macabre illusions offered up by effects of the magic lantern.[33] Lionel's image of the future at this point remains dark; represented only through the phantasmagoria, the entire earth becomes eclipsed by his dark imaginings. Remaining relatively uncontaminated by this unrestrained version of the imagination, Adrian assumes the mantle of action, volunteering to assume the protectorate of England. But still paralysed, Lionel can only see 'a vision of Adrian's form, tainted by pestilence, and sinking in death, float[ing]' before his eyes.[34] He attends a performance of Shakespeare's *Macbeth*, still seeking to escape the present, and notes approvingly that 'The wildness and supernatural machinery of Macbeth, was a pledge that it could contain little directly connected with our present circumstances.'[35] But his optimism of escapism is misplaced, for as the play unfolds, 'we gasped with [Macduff]' and, going even further than his fellow audience, Lionel admits that he 're-echoed the cry of Macduff and then rushed out as from an hell of torture, to find calm in the free air and silent street.'[36] Just as Frankenstein, Walton and the nameless creature have done before him, Lionel collapses the distinctions between representation and reality in a dangerous overindulgence of the imagination. The effects of the cauldron scene and the decrepitude of the hags are diminished, whilst the affect of the characters feeling 'the same passions that warmed our breasts' is augmented.[37]

The Last Man offers a particularly transformational and dynamic version of the Gothic, in showing its readership and its author the cathartic potential of horror and dread. But it also questions where the representational boundaries of those emotions should end. It is only as Lionel follows Adrian, and becomes an active agent who assists others, that he gradually learns to deal with those feelings. This entails a loss of radical subjectivity as he becomes part of a community. It is when Lionel takes his cue from Adrian's more selfless actions, assuming the plural pronoun of community, that he begins to appreciate the boundaries of the imagination, and move beyond the dire visions. Writing as part of that community, he later observes:

> Dire visions and evil auguries, if such things were, thickened around us, so that in vain might men say – These are their reasons, they are natural. We felt them to be ominous, and dreaded the future event enchained to them. That the night owl should screech before the noon-day sun, that the hard-winged bat should wheel around the bed

> of beauty, that muttering thunder should in early spring startle the cloudless air, that sudden and exterminating blight should fall on the tree and shrub, were unaccustomed, but physical events, less horrible than the mental creations of almighty fear. Some had sight of funeral processions, and faces all begrimed with tears, which flitted through the long avenues of the gardens, and drew aside the curtains of the sleepers at dead of night. Some heard wailing and cries in the air; a mournful chant would stream through the dark atmosphere, as if spirits above sang the requiem of the human race. What was there in all this, but that fear created other senses within our frames, making us see, hear, and feel what was not? What was this, but the action of diseased imaginations and childish credulity? So might it be; but what was most real, was the existence of these very fears; the staring looks of horror, the faces pale even to ghastliness, the voices struck dumb with harrowing dread, of those among us who saw and heard these things. We must go in change of scene, in occupation, and such security as we still hoped to find, we should discover a cure for those gathering horrors.[38]

'The mental creations of almighty fear' are finally appreciated for what they are by Lionel, who, whilst acknowledging their potency, resolves to gather everyone together in a quest 'to discover a cure for those gathering horrors'.

Whilst there is no immediate salvation, and the horrors do not dissipate, what is important, I think, is the way in which Lionel curbs and contains those horrors. Like Beatrice in *Valperga*, Lionel makes a conscious narratological decision not to extemporise too much on what the band of straggling survivors encounter as they cross the continent. In France, Lionel notes:

> Yet the last events that marked our progress through France were so full of strange horror and gloomy misery, that I dare not pause too long in the narration. If I were to dissect each incident, every small fragment of a second would contain an harrowing tale, whose minutest word would curdle the blood in thy young veins. It is right that I should erect for thy instruction this monument of the foregone race; but not that I should drag thee through the wards of an hospital, nor the secret chambers of the charnel-house. This tale, therefore, shall be rapidly unfolded.[39]

A meta-commentary on the much more detailed, horrific story of Victor Frankenstein, this passage also recalls the ghost of Hamlet's father in Shakespeare's play. The ghost's warning to Hamlet in Act I, scene V,

> I could a tale unfold whose lightest word
> Would harrow up thy soul, freeze thy young blood,
> Make thy two eyes, like stars, start from their spheres,
> Thy knotted and combined locks to part,
> And each particular hair to stand on end

is invoked here, only in order to be denied to the readership. Used also as an epigraph to Ann Radcliffe's novel *The Mysteries of Udolpho* (1794), 'I could a tale unfold' promises much, but its conditional tense is put to its true use here as Lionel rejects the full unfolding of that tale. The curbing of Lionel's story of terror continues as he later enters the city of Rome. Wandering through the empty city, Lionel recalls Ann Radcliffe again, this time her 1797 novel *The Italian*, observing that 'The romance with which, dipping our pencils in the rainbow hues of sky and transcendent nature, we to a degree gratuitously endow the Italians, replaced the solemn grandeur of antiquity. I remembered the dark monk, and floating figures of "The Italian" and how my boyish blood had thrilled at the description.'[40] Although on the one hand Lionel's textual approach to Rome suggests a persistence of indiscriminate reading, a reading that subsumes the reality, this passage indicates too the superior forces of romance over history and antiquity. He also demonstrates a sufficient self-awareness of his incursion into the region of romance, referring to how his 'boyish blood' had 'thrilled' at the description of the dark monk. As I noted in the Introduction, Mary had read Radcliffe's *The Italian* with pleasure in 1814. The pleasure and carefree nature of that reading is inscribed here as something that is definitively in the past.

As much as it is about apocalypse and environmental catastrophe, then, *The Last Man* also freights a consideration of the hermeneutics of horror and terror. It becomes a meditation on how we react to those forces. The horror of the physical, corporeal decay of the plague's victims is slowly replaced in the mind of Lionel by a dread of the future, and of what comes next. Whilst the novel warns that horror and terror are also contaminating forces that threaten to engulph their hosts, however, it gives us a character who survives to manage his dread, to contain his horror, and to face his future. '[I]t was with the utmost difficulty I kept myself free from the belief in supernatural events,' Lionel admits, but his laboured journey towards self-control is rewarded by him being able to tell his tale.

As the band of survivors reduces progressively, Adrian and Lionel remain to contemplate 'the glorious Alps, clothed in dazzling robes of light by the setting sun':

> Nature, or nature's favourite, this lovely earth, presented her most unrivalled beauties in resplendent and sudden exhibition. Below, far, far below, even as it were in the yawning abyss of the ponderous globe, lay the placid and azure expanse of lake Leman, vine-covered hills hedged it in, and behind dark mountains in cone-like shape, or irregular cyclopean wall, served for further defence. But beyond, and high above all, as if the spirits of the air had suddenly unveiled their bright abodes, placed in scaleless altitude in the stainless sky, heaven-kissing, companions of the unattainable ether, were the glorious Alps, clothed in dazzling robes of light by the setting sun. And, as if the world's wonders were never to be exhausted, their vast immensities, their jagged crags, and roseate painting, appeared again in the lake below, dipping their proud heights beneath the unruffled waves – palaces for the Naiads of the placid waters. Towns and villages lay scattered at the foot of Jura, which, with dark ravine, and black promontories, stretched its roots into the watery expanse beneath. Carried away by wonder, I forgot the death of man, and the living and beloved friend near me. When I turned, I saw tears streaming from his eyes; his thin hands pressed one against the other, his animated countenance beaming with admiration; 'Why' cried he, at last, 'Why, oh heart, whisperest thou of grief to me? Drink in the beauty of that scene, and possess delight beyond what a fabled paradise could afford.'[41]

The mouthpiece for the dearly departed Percy Bysshe Shelley, Adrian transmits a potent message about the management of grief, arguing for the laying aside of a 'fabled paradise' in favour of contemplating a present, majestic scene. In Adrian's invitation to 'drink in the beauty of that scene', it is possible to imagine a message from beyond the grave about the dynamic process of mourning. Mourning was a process that continued to preoccupy Mary Shelley in both her poetry and fiction. In 'The Choice', a poem that appears at the end of her journal of Sorrow, Mary swears to her dear departed Percy that 'My trembling hands shall never write thee – dead,' committing herself to keeping him alive through her writings.[42] A more intimate poem, composed in 1834 'To the Dead', pleads with him:

> O, Come to me in dreams, my Love,
> I will not ask a dearer bliss,
> Come with the starry beams, my Love,
> And press mine eyelids with thy kiss!'[43]

Here, in the passage from *The Last Man,* Adrian's 'animated countenance beaming with admiration' both idealises and memorialises Percy. The 'wonder' that Lionel experiences as he contemplates the wonders of the Alps with Adrian offers us a sanitised version of both characters' imagination. It is a version that privileges the Romantic ascendancy of the imagination, rather than the usurpation of that imagination through the congealing effects of horror. But placed as it is towards the end of the novel, its impermanency and fragility reveal that the Romantic imagination is more aspirational than possible. As Anne K. Mellor has argued, it is possible to read in Adrian's characterisation the flaws as well as the advantages of that particular type of imagination.[44] This is confirmed by Lionel's response to Adrian's invitation where he notes the consolatory, if temporary, effects of such 'enthusiastic transport, akin to happiness'.[45] In *The Last Man* the Romantic imagination offers temporary solace for the devastation of the world, but it is a sensation that is impermanent, fragile, and only 'akin' to happiness. Instead, the visceral experiences of dread, terror and horror prove to be the catalysts for transformation.

Having admitted their power, and then reined in the Gothic horrors that so consumed him, Lionel too can claim, alongside *Valperga*'s Euthanasia, that the present moment is all to him, as he 'drink[s] in the beauty' of what lies in front of him. Lionel Verney, the 'last man on earth' is explicitly associated with Mary Shelley through his exertions to curb the effects of horror and terror on his imagination, and his journey towards composing his own tale. But the gender of the author becomes more explicit in the Introduction to the tale, where Mary Shelley makes her editorial role explicit, informing her readership that she has edited the fragmentary leaves of a prophecy discovered in the cave of the Cumaean Sibyl that she visited with Shelley. That governing act of editorship provides a strong thematic link between *Frankenstein*, *Valperga* and *The Last Man*. As with Margaret Walton Saville and Euthanasia, we learn that the final authoritative manuscript comes from the pen of a female. The message concerning the transformative potential of the emotions of horror and terror, when these emotions are well managed, becomes all the sharper under such female editorship.

5

Terror, Horror and Transformation: The 1831 Edition of Frankenstein *and the Short Stories for* The Keepsake

> The reality of things began to dawn on my mind, bringing despair in its train. For several months I had been a prisoner: the evils of my dungeon had whipped my soul to madness, but they had subdued my corporeal frame. I was weak and wan. Torella had used a thousand artifices to administer to my comfort; I had detected and scorned them all – and I reaped the harvest of my obduracy.
>
> (Mary Shelley, 'Transformation', 1831)

'Transformation' is a key theme to the *oeuvre* of Mary Shelley. From the redemptive transformation of those of her characters who learn to control their emotions, to the dynamic transformational nature of Mary Shelley's engagement with different generic forms of the Gothic, both the themes and shape of her work suggest the importance of dynamic evolution.

The Fortunes of Perkin Warbeck, published in 1830, was the second historical novel that Mary Shelley composed. Although, unlike *Valperga*, there are no references to blood-curdling terror, in her sympathetic portrayal of the pretender to the English throne, and the narrative space awarded to Lady Katherine Gordon, Mary Shelley again seems to have taken her cue from other novelists who were formative to the Gothic tradition. Sophia Lee's free translation of Baculard d'Arnaud's *Warbeck* in her 1786 romance *Warbeck: A Pathetic Tale* also awarded considerable narrative space to the experiences and feelings of Lady Katherine Gordon.[1] This repositioning of the heroine was something that Mary Shelley, as I have argued, executed in some form or other in all of her work. Lady Katherine Gordon, as a forgotten female figure in history, offered the imaginative potential for the consideration of female experience in adversity.

While it is not possible within the remit or the space of this particular study to analyse *The Fortunes of Perkin Warbeck*, it is important to consider, nonetheless, the continuity between the publication of Mary Shelley's second historical novel, and her extensive revisions to *Frankenstein* for the ninth volume of Colburn and Bentley's Standard Novels Series in 1831. For we find that the revised edition of *Frankenstein* in 1831 offers a continuity in Mary Shelley's thinking on the combined themes of transformation and female experience. Although the transformations to the 1831 *Frankenstein* have already been relatively well documented, Mary Shelley's Preface to that particular edition nonetheless merits attention owing to the ways in which it sharpens the Gothic themes of terror and horror.[2] Whereas Percy Shelley's Preface to the first edition sought to distance *Frankenstein* from the Gothic tradition by hardly mentioning it at all, the 1831 Introduction by Mary Shelley capitalised on terror. It did so by drawing on the posthumous work of Ann Radcliffe, the author most explicitly associated with the female Gothic. Radcliffe's theorisation of terror and horror had been published after her death as 'On the Supernatural in Poetry' in the *New Monthly Magazine* in 1826. There, as I mentioned in the Introduction, drawing on Edmund Burke's theories of the sublime, Radcliffe had argued for the superiority of terror over horror, arguing that 'the first expands the soul, and awakens the faculties to a high degree of life', while the other, horror, 'contracts, freezes and nearly annihilates them'.[3] Radcliffe presents the appearance of the ghost in Shakespeare's *Hamlet* as a model of skilfully managed terror, arguing that

> Above every ideal being is the ghost of Hamlet, with all its attendant incidents of time and place. The dark watch on the remote platform, the dreary aspect of the night, the very expression of the officer on guard, 'the air bites shrewdly; it is very cold;' the recollection of a star, an unknown world, are all circumstances which excite forlorn,

> melancholy, and solemn feelings, and dispose us to welcome, with trembling curiosity, the awful being that draws near; and to indulge in that strange mixture of horror, pity, and indignation, produced by the tale it reveals.[4]

The 'incidents of time and place' only serve to complement the 'tale' that the ghost reveals, but they are crucial, in Radcliffe's view, to the indulgence of the 'strange mixture of horror, pity and indignation' that the readers experience. The *New Monthly Magazine* was owned by Henry Colburn, the publisher who also republished *Frankenstein* in 1831. Godwin had introduced Mary to Henry Colburn in the hope of gaining her some paid work, and Colburn obliged by publishing her essay 'Rome in the First and Nineteenth Centuries' in March 1824. We cannot say for sure whether Mary would have read Radcliffe's work in the *New Monthly Magazine*, but given her own earlier contributions to the same publication, there is a strong chance that she did. Mary Shelley's own technique in the 1831 Introduction to *Frankenstein* draws on Radcliffe's theorisation of terror. There, she reveals the minute circumstances of the 'wet, ungenial summer, and incessant rain' that confined herself, Shelley, Byron, Polidori and Claire Clairmont to the Villa Diodati. She further explicitly links the tale that she somewhat hazily remembered that they were reading from *Fantasmagoriana* to *Hamlet* through its similar use of attendant incidents of time and place:

> There was the *History of the Inconstant Lover*, who, when he thought to clasp the bride to whom he had pledged his vows, found himself in the arms of the pale ghost of her whom he had deserted. There was the tale of the sinful founder of his race whose miserable doom it was to bestow the kiss of death on all the younger sons of his fatal house, just when they reached the age of promise. His gigantic, shadowy form, clothed like the ghost in *Hamlet*, in complete armour, but with the beaver up, was seen at midnight, by the moon's fitful beams, to advance slowly along the gloomy avenue. The shape was lost beneath the castle walls, but soon a gate swung back, a step was heard, the door of the chamber opened, and he advanced to the couch of the blooming youths, cradled in healthy sleep.[5]

The level of detail awarded to the attendant incidents of time and place, and the comparison with the same scene from *Hamlet*, force one to conclude that Mary Shelley was drawing on the same lexicon and theorisation of terror that had been articulated in Radcliffe's 'On the Supernatural in Poetry'. Mary Shelley creates terror by recounting the story in such close detail as a *prelude* to describing what she sets as the preconditions for the ghost story that she seeks to invent as part of the competition, 'One which would speak to the mysterious fears of our nature and awaken thrilling horror – one to make the reader dread to look round, to curdle the blood, and quicken the beatings of the heart'.[6] The emphasis on physical sensation, fear and terror serve to galvanise the 'evil forebodings' in the reader that Walton ascribes to his sister Mrs Saville in the first letter. But Mary Shelley does not stop there in the Introduction; when she does finally come up with the idea for her ghost story 'with shut eyes, but acute mental vision', she takes her readership slowly over the contours of the story before admitting to being overcome by its terrors herself:

> I opened [my eyes] in terror. The idea so possessed my mind that a thrill of fear ran through me, and I wished to exchange the ghastly image of my fancy for the realities around. I see them still; the very room, the dark parquet, the closed shutters with the moonlight struggling through.[7]

This is a skilful Introduction to the novel; through recounting the genesis of her tale in such minute circumstances, paying attention to space, fitful sleep and a feeble moonlight, Mary Shelley creates an external scene of terror that unites both her and the readership more explicitly in a shared language of terror.

The changes made by Mary Shelley to the 1831 edition of *Frankenstein* testify to the author's increasing ease in acknowledging that she was working within an existent tradition of terror and horror. Whereas at the beginning of her writing career, she conceded the first Introduction of her novel to the pen of Percy Bysshe Shelley, in 1831 her account of its genesis moved away from the Romantic contexts towards the hypnagogic nightmare of waking terror. By 1831, Mary Shelley felt comfortable with acknowledging her use of an aesthetics of terror praised by Ann Radcliffe.

The changes do not stop there in 1831. They are also present in the transformations that she made to the novel itself. Her claim that these were merely 'stylistic' in the Introduction to this edition does not hold water. Elizabeth Lavenza's transformation from cousin of Victor Frankenstein to orphan fostered by his mother recalls the plot of many a female Gothic novel, and most particularly Eleanor Sleath's *The Orphan of the Rhine* (1798).[8] A peasant woman, who has raised Elizabeth when Frankenstein's mother first comes across her, states that she is the 'daughter of a Milanese nobleman. Her mother was a German and had died on giving her birth.'[9] Elizabeth's lineage recalls very closely that of Sleath's orphan heroine, but the textual change goes beyond merely paying tribute to her Gothic predecessors. If women's Gothic writing of the 1790s had illustrated all too forcefully the terrors of the disposability of the female, then this transformation underscores that concern. Victor Frankenstein's mother playfully presents the orphaned Elizabeth to Victor as a gift:

> On the evening previous to her being brought to my home, my mother had said playfully, 'I have a pretty present for my Victor – tomorrow he shall have it.' And when, on the morrow, she presented Elizabeth to me as her promised gift, I, with childish seriousness, interpreted her words literally and looked on Elizabeth as mine – mine to protect, love and cherish. All praises bestowed on her I received as made to a possession of my own. We called each other familiarly by the name of cousin. No word, no expression could body forth the kind of relation in which she stood to me – my more than sister, since till death she was to be mine only.[10]

Frankenstein's arrogant certainty of his possession of Elizabeth 'till death', encouraged by his mother's own casual, thoughtless approach to the disposal of Elizabeth, anticipates the bloody demise of Elizabeth at the hands of his creature. From the moment that she enters into the sphere of his life as 'a child fairer than a pictured cherub' she becomes his to dispose of as he wishes. In Chapter 2 of the 1831 edition, Elizabeth continues to be moulded more closely in the conventions of the Gothic heroine, for here Mary Shelley extemporises further on Elizabeth's love of sublime nature. Her 'following the aerial creations of the poets' is supplemented by her 'admiration and delight' in 'the sublime shapes of the mountains, the changes of the seasons, tempest and calm, the silence of winter, and the life and turbulence of our Alpine summers'.[11] Elizabeth comes to be represented more fully in this revised edition in the mould of Mary's 1823 heroine Euthanasia, who also discovers the most pleasure and solace from her moments of solitude in the mountains that surround her castle. Elizabeth's careful appreciation of the changing seasons, the 'silence of winter', is diminished in Victor's account to her appreciating 'the magnificent appearances of things', taking a poor second place to his superior investigation of 'their causes'. But his superior arrogation of divine, Promethean power leads only to death and destruction, pulling Elizabeth Lavenza in its wake.

Elizabeth's closer assimilation in the 1831 edition to the Gothic heroine and to her earlier prototype, Euthanasia, both in terms of her orphaned status, her immediate possession by the male usurper and her appreciation of landscape, lend the 1831 edition of *Frankenstein* a sharper edge of critique, one that is more explicitly crafted through the ongoing preoccupations of Mary Shelley with the Gothic disposability of the female in *Valperga* and *The Last Man*. Yet still it speaks to the silences within *Frankenstein*; Elizabeth's voice remains stifled in the paratextual layers, her letters possibly mutilated by Victor Frankenstein as he recounts them to Walton. Her own story is never revealed, but in its fragmented, partial retelling through the mouthpiece of Victor Frankenstein, its details, narrated at such an early juncture in the novel, become a crucial incident in Mary Shelley's carefully constructed story of terror. *Frankenstein* in 1818 offered in its pages a tale of terror, but its mediation of that selfsame blood-curdling terror in the later 1831 edition is more incisive and terrifying.

Mary Shelley's increasing ease with 'blood-curdling terror' and Gothic precursors is realised most fully in her short story 'Transformation', published in the literary annual *The Keepsake* in 1831. Shelley had several items published in *The Keepsake* both in 1831 and in other years. *The Keepsake* was an annual gift book, a luxury item bound in silk that was designed to grace drawing room tables across England. George Eliot ventriloquises the scorn in which many men held such publications through her character Tertius

Lydgate in *Middlemarch*. As Rosamond Vincy's unfortunate and unfavoured suitor Ned Plymdale brings her a copy as a gift, Lydgate voices a particularly masculine scorn of such publications:

> [Ned Plymdale] had brought the last 'Keepsake,' the gorgeous watered-silk publication which marked modern progress at that time; and he considered himself very fortunate that he could be the first to look over it with [Rosamond], dwelling on the ladies and gentlemen with shiny copper-plate cheeks and copper-plate smiles, and pointing to comic verses as capital and sentimental stories as interesting. Rosamond was gracious, and Mr. Ned was satisfied that he had the very best thing in art and literature as a medium for 'paying addresses' – the very thing to please a nice girl [. . .] 'What are you laughing at so profanely?' said Rosamond, with bland neutrality. 'I wonder which would turn out to be the silliest – the engravings or the writing here,' said Lydgate, in his most convinced tone, while he turned over the pages quickly, seeming to see all through the book in no time, and showing his large white hands to much advantage, as Rosamond thought.[12]

The Keepsake, in its luxury binding, was viewed as an economic status symbol rather than a volume of serious literary endeavour. And yet, if one looks over the contents of the 1831 volume, it is easy to see how Mary Shelley's short story 'Transformation' is anomalous. Placed among poems, and other short stories, Shelley's haunting tale of a proud young man who is tempted by a diabolical dwarf to swap bodies with him stands out. Like Victor Frankenstein, the father of Matilda, Castruccio and the young Lionel Verney, Shelley's character Guido is proud and aggressive:

> I was born with the most imperious, haughty, tameless spirit, with which every mortal was gifted. I quailed before my father only; and he, generous and noble, but capricious and tyrannical, at once fostered and checked the wild impetuosity of my character, making obedience necessary, but inspiring no respect for the motives which guided his commands.[13]

Reiterating the necessity for careful education and guidance, Guido's father, like many other father figures in Mary Shelley's *oeuvre*, does not do enough to check the 'haughty' spirit of his son. As Guido's father dies, another surrogate father figure takes his place, the Marquis of Torella, whose patience and goodness with the impetuous, uncaring Guido is almost beyond belief. Yet Guido's 'tameless spirit' will not brook patience; he both wants Torella's daughter Juliet as his beloved bride, and yet expects her to wait as he explores the extremes of hedonistic masculinity. Guido's hedonism is similar to Victor Frankenstein's careless negligence of Elizabeth Lavenza; his betrothed Juliet, narrated only through his viewpoint, becomes another object of possession, similar to Elizabeth Lavenza:

> [Torella] sent for his daughter – he presented me to her as her betrothed. The chamber became hallowed by a holy light as she entered. Hers was that cherub look, those large soft eyes, full dimpled cheeks, and mouth of infantine sweetness, that expresses the rare union of happiness and love. Admiration first possessed me; she is mine! was the second proud emotion, and my lips curled with haughty triumph.[14]

A pleasing object to possess, Juliet only becomes something to prize when she is at risk of being possessed by another man. When Guido's hedonistic pursuits convince him that he has lost Juliet, his only regret seems to be that 'Another would call her his!'[15] She is yet another silent form who at first seems to lurk only in the margins of the tale. Nevertheless, it is worth noting that, perhaps because of the publication's intended female audience, what the literary annual chose to engrave was an image of Juliet, not an image of the horrific agent of Beelzebub who comes to exchange bodies with Guido.

The dwarf's grotesque features are described in detail by Guido as he first witnesses him on the sea shore. Again, paying lipservice to Ann Radcliffe's advice concerning the evocation of terror, Mary Shelley sets the scene carefully for Guido's encounter of the dwarf on the beach:

> Evening was at hand, when, seaward, arose, as if on the waving of a wizard's wand, a murky web of clouds, blotting the late azure sky, and darkening and disturbing the till now placid deep. The clouds had strange fantastic shapes; and they changed, and mingled, and seemed to be driven about by a mighty spell.[16]

The dwarf that Guido then encounters on the beach has 'squinting eyes, distorted features, and body deformed till it became a horror to hold'.[17] His voice is 'screeching and wretched'. Yet within the space of this story, he is the only one to listen to Guido, and to counsel him on his morals. Guido exchanges bodies with the dwarf in the hope of pursuing his careless pleasures. The dwarf breaks the pact that he swap bodies with Guido for three days and nights, and in fact wanders off to possess Juliet himself. Guido, in the body of the dwarf, eventually realises that he has been duped, and proceeds to go and find the dwarf, and swap back his body.

'Transformation' is a story which defies Gothic convention while playing with those selfsame conventions. Unlike Lewis's *The Monk* and Charles Robert Maturin's *Melmoth the Wanderer*, both of which had been published earlier, Mary Shelley's 'Transformation' does not resolve itself with the eternal damnation of the central character Guido. Rather, he is allowed to repent, regain his own mortal frame, and marry Juliet, sadder but wiser:

> as the benevolent and generous Torella sat beside me, talking such wisdom as might win friends to repentance, and mine own dear Juliet hovered near me, administering to my wants, and cheering me by her smiles, the work of my bodily cure and mental reform went on well together. Juliet sometimes ventures to allude bitterly to the malice that caused this change, but I kiss her on the moment, and tell her all is for the best. I am a fonder and more faithful husband – and true is this – but for that wound, never had I called her mine. [18]

Guido's temporary exchange of bodies with the dwarf is what, effectively, rouses him to become a husband, to leave the homosocial hedonistic world of masculine pleasures and to marry his beloved. As a female character, Juliet seems at first glance to be another insubstantial female figure, one who waits patiently in the wings for her betrothed to reform and return to her. However, there is one small but substantial qualification to this judgement. The conclusion to this odd tale recounts that after marriage, Juliet would advert 'bitterly to the malice that caused this change'.[19] We remain unsure as to what, precisely, Juliet knows of the body exchange, but that adverb 'bitterly' sits uneasily here, retaining, as it does, the trace of a feminist criticism of Guido's behaviour.

The doubles that haunted the tale of *Frankenstein*, relegating the females to the margins of the novel, are also at the heart of 'Transformation', containing, as it does, the tale of one diabolical male attempting to possess the body of another. Despite the angelic illustration of Juliet in the pages of *The Keepsake*, 'Transformation' sits uneasily in this compendium of luxury literary fragments with its narrative of male pride, hedonism and negligence. Perhaps, however, the grains of its critique lie too within its framework; Guido is allowed to live happily ever after with his Juliet, whereas Elizabeth Lavenza dies. Juliet, however, is permitted to be bitter about Guido's 'transformation'.

'Transformation' is just one example of many short stories that illustrate how supple and nuanced Mary Shelley's aesthetics of terror and horror were, and how they evolved in response to the economic demands placed on her. Whilst the 1831 edition of *Frankenstein* rendered the critique of the scientist and adventurer more explicit in its rendition of 'bloodcurdling terror', 'Transformation' played with the iconography of the tale of terror, paying close attention to circumstances, male arrogance reformed, and the near-silent heroine that lies at its heart. Thematically, it is interesting to note the prevalence of this theme of male arrogance and reformation throughout the fiction of Mary Shelley. That theme maps quite closely onto 'The Spectre Barber' by J. Musäus that had appeared in Eyriès's *Fantasmagoriana* read by the group assembled at the Villa Diodati in 1816. Francis, the protagonist of that story, as a young man, is ruined by his immense inheritance and becomes dissipated too, suggesting that the genesis of this theme was present from the very beginnings of Mary Shelley's writing career.

Hypermasculinity, dissipation and reform continued to be a lifelong preoccupation for Mary Shelley. 'The Mortal Immortal: A Tale', which she contributed to the 1833 *Keepsake* retained this theme in its portrayal of a young man who is the pupil of the sixteenth-century alchemist Cornelius Agrippa. Agrippa had of course been mentioned in *Frankenstein* as one of Victor's key sources of inspiration in his quest to create new life. Here, however, Agrippa's power is somewhat diminished by the form that the tale assumes. There is a skittishness to its tone that deflates its potential Gothic charge. The narrative assumes the form of a dramatic monologue; its narrator, the 'mortal immortal' takes the tone of an antiquarian. 'The Wandering Jew?' he asks of his readership in the second paragraph, only to reply, 'Certainly not. More than eighteen centuries have passed over his head. In comparison with him, I am a very young immortal.'[20] He then proceeds to deviate from his story by anxiously examining a grey hair that he has discovered on his head, hoping that its presence tends towards symptoms of ageing. In the form of the dramatic monologue again, he catches his digression and reins himself in with the phrase 'But to my task.' 'All the world has heard of Cornelius Agrippa,' the narrator confidently asserts, claiming with no modesty that 'His memory is as immortal as his arts have made me. All the world has also heard of his scholar, who, unawares, raised the foul fiend during his master's absence, and was destroyed by him.'[21] Cornelius Agrippa, in this tale, comes across through the narrator Winzy's focalisation as a benign, elderly gentleman who is careful of his pupil's safety, warning him not to drink from the alembics which contain his alchemical experimentation. But Winzy, desirous of securing the hand of his beloved Bertha who seems to him to have shown a preference for another, Albert, decides that he will defy the injunction of Agrippa:

> And he slept. His venerable head sunk on his breast, and I scarce heard his regular breathing. For a few minutes I watched the vessel – the rosy hue of the liquid remained unchanged. Then my thoughts wandered – they visited the fountain, and dwelt on a thousand charming scenes never to be renewed – never! Serpents and adders were in my heart as the word 'Never!' half formed itself on my lips. False girl! – false and cruel! Never more would she smile on me as that evening she smiled on Albert. Worthless, detested woman! I would not remain unrevenged – she should see Albert expire at her feet – she should die beneath my vengeance. She had smiled in disdain and triumph – she knew my wretchedness and her power. Yet what power had she? The power of exciting my hate – my utter scorn – oh, all but indifference! Could I attain that – could I regard her with careless eyes, transferring my rejected love to one fairer and more true, that were indeed a victory! [22]

Winzy's decision to drink from the alembic is due to his loss of emotional control. There is a hatred of Bertha in this, as he imagines her death, and that of the hapless Albert. Winzy, it transpires, is wrong: Bertha has always been true to him, and there is no textual evidence to suggest that the 'old high-born hag' who is the guardian of Bertha has anything against Winzy. He marries Bertha, but his punishment is to see her fade and die, as he continues to remain youthful. Again, the engraving that accompanied the story in *The Keepsake* retained its focus on the untold female story. Painted by Henry P. Briggs and engraved by Frederick Bacon, 'Bertha' shows in the centre of the picture a fading elderly lady with a walking stick, with a youthful Winzy relegated firmly to the shade of the left side of the picture. Intentionally or not, *The Keepsake* kept promoting the untold female narratives that trouble and disturb the passion-fraught, arrogant and overreaching accounts offered by the hypermasculine narrators.

'Transformation' and 'The Mortal Immortal', in their focus on physical metamorphoses, show to us the frail, and possibly impermanent nature of the spiritual repentance that their male narrators claim. They are distinctly different in tone and form from *Frankenstein*, *Matilda*, *Valperga* and *The Last Man*. Whereas in their form they may contain more of the fantastic, offering accounts as they do of impossible physical transformations which involve grotesque dwarves and alchemical potions, in tone both tales seek to reduce the Gothic charge of their narratives. In so doing, they illustrate a sharper edge of critique than what had gone before in Mary Shelley's fiction, for they point up the arrogance and folly of their male narrators.

Conclusion

> I should advise you, by the bye – not to read my novel –You will not like it – I cannot *teach* – I can only *paint*, such as my paintings are –
>
> (Mary Wollstonecraft Shelley, letter to Edward John Trelawny, Thursday 26 January 1837)

Referring to her final published novel *Falkner* (1837), Mary Shelley insisted in a letter to Edward Trelawny that she could 'only *paint*'. Her comment is of interest for its emphasis on what she perceived as a shortcoming in her work. 'I cannot *teach*,' she first protested, as if her painterly skills were a poor substitute for the preferred quality of didacticism. An author whose career had spanned three decades, who had composed seven novels, one novella, numerous essays, short stories, poems, memoirs, histories, and who had served as editor to the poetry of Lord Byron and, posthumously, her husband Percy Bysshe Shelley, Mary Shelley remained profoundly aware of what her writing did not do. It did not seek to teach, to inculcate morals, because for her the crux of her art lay in placing faith in the rational judgement of her readership. From the complex narrative frame of *Frankenstein*, which forces us to interrogate the sincerity of Victor Frankenstein's hope to 'enlarge [the] faculties and understanding' of Robert Walton, to the silent editorships of the narratives in *Matilda*, *Valperga* and *The Last Man*, Mary Shelley encourages us, her readers, to judge aright for ourselves as we consider how and why these tales are delivered to us.[1]

Frequently, there is the figure of a female artist within Mary Shelley's narratives. Female artists were also at the heart of many of

Ann Radcliffe's novels, in particular in the characterisations of the heroines Julia di Mazzini in *A Sicilian Romance* (1790) and Ellena di Rosalba in *The Italian* (1797). But whereas in Radcliffe's works these heroines and their artistic endeavours were placed at the very opening of the romances, Mary Shelley's figuration of the female artist was more deeply embedded within the layers of her tales. Their presence was, nevertheless, of equal significance. Here, we might consider how Elizabeth Lavenza in *Frankenstein* paints with quiet satisfaction, how Perdita in *The Last Man* draws to please herself rather than others. These female artists paint with no greater aim than their own gratification. In them we see an aspect of how Mary Shelley viewed her own craft. To paint sympathy, friendship, folly, ambition and ungoverned passions was infinitely more rewarding to both the author and her readership than any vainglorious attempt to teach moral rectitude.

The majority of Mary Shelley's fiction offers us characters who come to terms with their passions, reining in as they so do their own experiences of terror and horror. There is Matilda's refusal to revel in absolute horror in the wake of her father's suicide, Beatrice's decision not to reveal the extent of the horrors of her abduction, rape and imprisonment to Euthanasia in *Valperga*, Lionel Verney's success in governing his own feelings of terror and horror in *The Last Man* and, of course, the silent, rational editorship of *Frankenstein* by Margaret Walton Saville. And while the short stories 'Transformation' and 'The Mortal Immortal' are decidedly different in tone from the longer narratives, they nonetheless point up the transformative capacity of their male characters.

'The Bride of Modern Italy', which Mary Shelley published in *The London Magazine* in April 1824, is, however, somewhat different in emphasis. It is a vivid, and, one is tempted to say, bitter, painting of the fates of young women who must depend on their fathers, or on the Church, to decide their fates. The central protagonist Clorinda was, as Betty T. Bennett and Charles E. Robinson have noted, based on Emilia Viviani.[2] When the Shelleys met her in Pisa, they found a young woman immured in a convent passively awaiting the arrangement of her marriage. Emily W. Sunstein observes that '[Percy] Shelley was enraptured by this beautiful victim and fell patently in love, just as Mary came to know her well enough to see that she was rather common, quite worldly-wise beneath her effusive rhetoric, and acting a romantic part with him.'[3] Tempting though it may be to think that under such difficult personal circumstances 'The Bride of Modern Italy' is an excoriation of its female protagonist, this is not the case. Mary Shelley's painterly eye in this short story directs the interpretative perspective of her reader, advising that reader to banish all preconceptions about convents in Italy. The opening to the tale directs the reader down an overgrown garden path in the convent of 'Saint S —':

> [The reader] must figure it to himself as bounded by a long, low, straggling, white-washed, weather-stained building, with grated windows, the lower ones glassless. It is a kitchen garden, but the refuse of the summer stock alone remained, except a few cabbages, which perfumed the air with their rank exhalations. The walks were neglected, yet not overgrown, but strewed with broken earthen-ware, ashes, cabbage-stalks, orange-peel, bones, and all that marks the vicinity of a much frequented, but disorderly mansion.[4]

Chaotic, repugnant, the convent's garden mirrors the 'disorderly mansion'. The inhabitants, customs and food of that 'mansion' are painted with clear scorn by the narrator; the nourishment, for example, consists of 'cellars of black salt; bottles of sour wine, and small loaves of bitter bread'.[5] The disordered botanical imagery of the garden recalls Mary Wollstonecraft's promotion of female enlightenment over luxuriant decay in *A Vindication of the Rights of Woman* (1792). Clorinda, the 'Bride of Modern Italy', is a young woman whose enforced conventual existence leads to her own luxuriant decay. The closet in her cell is painted for the reader in considerable detail:

> [In] a closet, with the door a-jar, among tattered books and female apparel, hung a glass-case enclosing a waxen Gesu Bambino, and some flowers, gathered for this holy dedication and drooping for want of light, were placed beneath him; some mignonette, basil, and heliotrope, weeds o'ergrown, flowered in a wooden trough at the window; a broken looking-glass; a leaden ink stand – such was Clorinda's boudoir.[6]

The claustrophobia of the boudoir is palpable. The description of its neglected objects aims to arouse disgust and condemnation in the reader in a manner that is far more radically explicit than many of Mary Shelley's other works. Here, the interpretative and symbolic layers of her other fictions are stripped away, leaving a stagnant atmosphere beyond hope of ventilation and rejuvenation. The subsequent characterisation of Clorinda herself, fretting over whether a suitor will materialise to rescue her from her imprisonment, shows that she too is beyond redemption. Too long a product of the disordered convent, Clorinda wavers in purpose, favouring one lover over another only in the hope that he will prove to be the chivalrous knight in shining armour destined to save her. The chaos of the convent mirrors the disorder of Clorinda's thinking. Unlike the Gothic heroines of Ann Radcliffe who were immured in convents in *A Sicilian Romance* and *The Italian*, Clorinda exhibits no inner resourcefulness, no fidelity and no capacity for artistry. The condemnation of such female passivity is, to say the least, trenchant. Her conduct embodies the absolute antithesis of the rationality that Mary Wollstonecraft had urged women to cultivate in *A Vindication of the Rights of Woman*.

The tale of 'The Bride of Modern Italy' offers a prototype for Mary Shelley's later works in the 1830s. It provokes a disgust that plays with, but never quite reaches, the borders of abject horror. Terror and horror, Mary Shelley resolved, were not the most agile aesthetics in the 1830s for the sharpening of her writing on female education and independence. While, as I argued in Chapter 5, on the one hand Mary Shelley intensified the Gothic dynamics of *Frankenstein* in her 1831 edition of the novel, her later works of the 1830s marked a decided departure from the Gothic aesthetics of terror and horror.

It was, however, as early as 1831 that Mary Shelley began to compose *Lodore*, a novel that she described in her letters as ready for publication towards the close of 1833.[7] Unlike *Frankenstein*'s carefully imprecise setting of 17—, *Valperga* and *The Fortunes of Perkin Warbeck*'s meticulously researched historical settings and the futuristic visions of the twenty-first century in *The Last Man*, *Lodore* is set in the early 1830s during which it was composed. Moving between the mores of cosmopolitan London, the allure of fashionable Naples, the wilds of Illinois, New York and the Niagara Falls and Rome, this tale of a daughter's miseducation and an absent mother has often been read more as being commercially consonant with the silver-fork novels that were published in great numbers by Mary's publisher Henry Colburn.[8] The generic vehicle and contemporaneous setting for *Lodore* were indeed different, but then such experimentation was nothing new for Mary Shelley. What remained the same were the themes of the novel. These involved a preoccupation with the education of daughters, and the consequences of a misguided education. These were themes that ran, as I have argued in the course of this book, through almost all of Mary Shelley's works. Explored through different generic forms, Mary Shelley took pains both to expose the dangerous consequences of deficient educations, and to demonstrate the potential for the reversal of these dangerous consequences through the transformative experiences of female friendship. Empathy and female friendship are the qualities most clearly valorised in *Lodore*. They are strikingly absent in the figure of this novel's Clorinda, the first Italian bride of Arthur Saville who is clearly modelled on the earlier Clorinda from 'The Bride of Modern Italy'. They are also lacking in the naïve, young Lady Lodore, who at the insinuations of her mother, abandons her infant, without a fight, to the hands of her affectionate but impetuous father, who takes the child off to be reared in the wilds of Illinois. This infant becomes the heroine Ethel, but she is a heroine whose educational shortcomings, emotional inarticulacy and superhuman faith in her male protectors are painted with ruthless scrutiny. Her education is discovered to be particularly deficient when compared with that of her friend and supporter Fanny Derham. Fanny, an early model, perhaps, for Charlotte Brontë's later independent heroine Shirley, confesses to loving Plato, Cicero and Epictetus, and acknowledges that studying these authors removes her from more worldly considerations. The differences between her education by her father and that of Ethel by Lord Lodore is foregrounded in the novel:

> Each had been the favourite daughter of men of superior qualities of mind. They had been educated by their several fathers with the most sedulous care, and nothing could be more opposite than the result, except that, indeed, both made duty the master motive of their actions.

> Ethel had received, so to speak, a sexual education. Lodore had formed his ideal of what a woman ought to be, of what he wished to find his wife, and sought to mould his daughter accordingly. Mr. Derham contemplated the duties and objects befitting an immortal soul, and had educated his child for the performances of them. The one fashioned his offspring to be the wife of a frail human being, and instructed her to be yielding, and to make it her duty to devote herself to his happiness, and to obey his will. The other sought to guard his from all weakness, to make her complete in herself, and to render her independent and self-sufficing.[9]

The consequences of such differing educations are clear. Fanny is 'independent', whereas Ethel is reliant first on her father, and then on her husband, Villiers. The misguided attempts, or absence of, paternal education is a theme that ran throughout Mary Shelley's work, from Victor Frankenstein's father misguidedly leaving him to his own devices, to Matilda's father neglecting her education, to Euthanasia, the independent, rational heroine of *Valperga* being trained classically by her father. But here the issue becomes more personal and urgent. 'We feel the evil results of our own faults,' the narrator warns, 'and endeavour to guard our children from them; forgetful that the opposite extreme also has its peculiar dangers.'[10]

But like the friendship between Euthanasia and Beatrice in *Valperga*, empathy and female friendship become the redemptive qualities of *Lodore*. While Fanny Derham may be self-sufficing, she nonetheless offers sympathetic friendship to Ethel, and to Ethel's mother. The dangers and consequences of fathers educating daughters are highlighted in both *Lodore* and in the later *Falkner* (1837), as Mary Shelley presents us with resourceful female characters in both works who create strong female bonds. Through those bonds in *Lodore*, the absent mother is rescued and reintroduced into the family towards the end of the novel. While critics have concentrated on the possible conservatism of these two final works, there is something to be said, too, for their continuance of the preoccupations in Mary Shelley's earlier works, and for their radicalisation of family groups. The absent mother was a frequent trope of Gothic fiction, from Julia di Mazzini rediscovering and rescuing her mother in Ann Radcliffe's *A Sicilian Romance* through the strongly supportive friendship that she has forged with her mentor Madame de Menon, to Ellena di Rosalba in *The Italian* rediscovering her presumed dead mother through her earlier forging of a friendship with her. The theme permeated many works of Gothic fiction beyond Radcliffe too, most particularly in Maria Regina Roche's *The Children of the Abbey* (1794). The figure of the absent, but rediscovered mother is not conservative; her discovery and rehabilitation are effected through the radical, supportive dynamics of female friendship.

In *Falkner* (1837), the heroine Elizabeth is the adopted daughter of Rupert Falkner, who pays him 'a child's duty' in gratitude for his adoption of her. When her adoptive father is arrested on suspicion of murder, it is expected that Elizabeth will renounce him in order to escape the ignominy of the charge. But she does not; standing by her adoptive father, she celebrates as positive qualities the 'gratitude, obedience, duty' that she owes to him, defying societal expectations that she will abandon him. The judgement of the young independent heroine becomes a matter of pride, reaffirming the author's faith in the sanctity of individual judgement.

If, in her final works, *Lodore* and *Falkner*, Mary Shelley abandoned the aesthetics of terror and horror, she did not entirely dispense with the tropes of the Gothic. By the 1830s, in the wake of repeated satires from the pens of Thomas Love Peacock, Jane Austen and others, Gothic was wrongly viewed as being outmoded; irrelevant even. As a form it was commercially less viable in the age of the silver-fork novel. Nevertheless, the focus on female experience, independence, friendship, parental bonds and education that was so important to the early Gothic works of the 1790s persisted in the later works of Mary Shelley.

The Gothic as a form is heterogeneous, involving a range of tropes which resurface again and again. It investigates, absorbs and reflects critically on the dominant debates of its times. The same can be said for the remarkable *oeuvre* of Mary Wollstonecraft Shelley. Absorbing a wide range of learned sources, questioning familial and educational dynamics, her work is never scornful of her literary predecessors. The fictional forms may have changed for Mary Shelley towards the close of her career, but the themes remained the same. The curbing of the passions, the capacity for transformation, the dynamics of female friendships and familial relations are the deep veins of connection that run through her writing. As readers of Gothic and Romanticism, we do well to recognise and appreciate the continuation and transformation of those preoccupations across a fuller range of her work. Mary Wollstonecraft Shelley was much, much more than the sum of the parts of *Frankenstein*.

Notes

Introduction

[1] Tilottama Rajan, Introduction to Mary Shelley, *Valperga* (1823) (Peterborough, ON: Broadview Press), p. 11.

[2] Nora Crook, 'Mary Shelley, Author of *Frankenstein*', in *A Companion to the Gothic*, ed. David Punter (Oxford: Blackwell, 2000), pp. 8–69. Crook notes here that 'It is often assumed that Mary Shelley's demonic, Gothic side exhausted itself with *Frankenstein*, but Gothic romance continued to punctuate her life' (p. 63).

[3] On the initially lukewarm reception and popularity of *Frankenstein*, William St Clair has observed that 'for the first fourteen years of its life in print *Frankenstein* existed in about a thousand copies, fewer than most of the works of Byron and Scott sold on publication day' (St Clair, *The Reading Nation in the Romantic Period* (Cambridge: Cambridge University Press, 2004), p. 365). His study also includes a good appendix on the publication history of the novel and its adaptations.

[4] Mary Wollstonecraft Shelley to Leigh Hunt, 9 September 1823, in *The Letters of Mary Wollstonecraft Shelley*, ed. Betty T. Bennett, 2 vols (Baltimore and London: The Johns Hopkins University Press, 1980), vol. I, p. 378.

5 The second edition of *Frankenstein* arranged by Godwin was published in 1823 by G. and W. B. Whittaker. Mary Shelley had no say whatsoever in its production, but she did retain the revisions that Godwin made to this edition in her later 1831 edition. For further information on this, see Nora Crook, ed. *Frankenstein; or, The Modern Prometheus,* introd. Betty T. Bennett, in *The Novels and Selected Works of Mary Shelley,* vol. 1. (London: William Pickering, 1996), xcvi.

6 Betty T. Bennett and Charles E. Robinson (ed.), Preface to *The Mary Shelley Reader* (Oxford: Oxford University Press, 1990), p. vii.

7 Mary Shelley, Author's Introduction to the Colburn and Bentley Standard Novels Edition of *Frankenstein, or the Modern Prometheus* (1831), ed. Maurice Hindle (Harmondsworth: Penguin, 1985), p. 55.

8 In relation to this, see Vivien Jones, 'The Death of Mary Wollstonecraft', *British Journal for Eighteenth-Century Studies,* 20/2 (1997), 187–205.

9 On the courtship of William Godwin and Mary Jane Clairmont, see chapter 18, 'The Second Mrs Godwin', of William St Clair's *The Godwins and the Shelleys: The Biography of a Family* (London: Faber and Faber, 1989), pp. 238–54.

10 [Mary Wollstonecraft], Review of *The Italian, The Analyical Review: Or, History of Literature*, 25/5 (May 1797), 516–20. For further information on this, see Dale Townshend and Angela Wright, 'Gothic and Romantic Engagements', in Dale Townshend and Angela Wright (eds), *Ann Radcliffe, Romanticism and the Gothic* (Cambridge: Cambridge University Press, 2014), p. 11.

11 For further insight into Godwin's organic process of writing the weighty *Enquiry Concerning Political Justice,* see William St Clair's chapter entitled 'Writing a Masterpiece' in *The Godwins and the Shelleys*, pp. 55–68.

12 Mary Shelley, Author's Introduction, in *Frankenstein* (1831).

13 Emily W. Sunstein, *Mary Shelley: Romance and Reality* (Baltimore: The Johns Hopkins University Press, 1989), p. 42.

14 Mary Shelley, *Mounseer Nongtongpaw; or, the Discoveries of John Bull in a Trip to Paris.* (London: Proprietors of the Juvenile Library [M. J. Godwin & Co.], 1808.

15 Percy Bysshe Shelley to Thomas Jefferson Hogg, 3 [for 4] October 1814, in *Percy Bysshe Shelley Letters*, vol. I, p. 402, quoted in Sunstein, *Mary Shelley*, p. 72.

16 *The Journals of Mary Shelley, 1814–1844*, ed. Paula R. Feldman and Diana Scott-Kilvert (Oxford: Clarendon Press, 1987), vol. 1, p. 28.

[17] On the controversial reception of *The Monk,* see Michael Gamer, 'Genres for the Prosecution: Pornography and the Gothic', *PMLA*, 114/5 (1999). 1043–54, and my chapter on Matthew Lewis in Angela Wright, *Britain, France and the Gothic, 1764–1820: The Import of Terror* (Cambridge: Cambridge University Press, 2013), pp.135–41.

[18] Samuel Taylor Coleridge, Review of *The Monk* in the *Critical Review*, 19 (February 1797), 194–200, quoted in E. J. Clery and Robert Miles (eds), *Gothic Documents: A Sourcebook 1700–1820* (Manchester: Manchester University Press, 2000), p. 187.

[19] Mary Shelley, 'On Ghosts', *London Magazine*, 9 (March 1824): 253–56; repr, in Bennett and Robinson (eds), *The Mary Shelley Reader*, pp. 334–40; p. 334.

[20] Edmund Burke, *A Philosophical Enquiry into the Origin of our Ideas of the Sublime and Beautiful* (1757), ed. David Womersley (London: Penguin, 1998), p. 86.

[21] Nathan Drake, *Literary Hours or Setches Critical and Narrative,* XV (Sudbury, 1798), p. 246.

[22] Drake, *Literary Hours*, p. 246.

[23] Drake, *Literary Hours*, p. 246.

[24] Mary Shelley, Diary entry for Sunday 27 November 1814 in *The Journals of Mary Shelley*, vol. I, p. 48.

[25] See the reading list for 1814 in *The Journals of Mary Shelley*, vol. 1, pp.85–7.

[26] See the reading list for 1815, in *The Journals of Mary* Shelley, vol. 1, pp. 88–91.

[27] See, for example, Paul Sherwin, '*Frankenstein:* Creation as Catastrophe', *PMLA*, 96/5 (1981), 883–903; William Veeder, *Mary Shelley and* Frankenstein: *The Fate of Androgyny* (Chicago: University Press of Chicago, 1986), 143; Jerrold E Hogle, for one, provides a corrective to these readings in his essay '*Frankenstein* as neo-gothic: from the ghost of the counterfeit to the monster of abjection', in Tiilottama Rajan and Julia M. Wright (eds), *Romanticism, History and the Possibilities of Genre* (Cambridge: Cambridge University Press, 1998), pp. 176–212. Hogle argues for *Frankenstein*'s roots in the Gothic of Horace Walpole going very 'deep indeed' and that it 'redeployed the Gothic mode on the basis of the most basic presuppositions underlying the Gothic itself' (p. 178).

[28] William Godwin, writing as [Edward Baldwin], *The Pantheon, or Ancient*

History of the Gods of Greece and Rome (London: 1806). See chapter X in particular.

29 E. J. Clery, *Women's Gothic* (Tavistock: Northcote House, 2000), p. 125.

30 Gillen d'Arcy Wood, *Tambora: The Eruption that Changed the World* (Princeton and Oxford: Princeton University Press, 2014).

31 Jean-Baptiste Eyriès, *Fantasmagoriana, ou receuil d'histoires d'apparitions de spectres, revenans, fantômes etc.* (Paris: F. Schoell, 1812). I am grateful to Maximilien van Woundenberg of the Sheridan Institute of Technology for sharing his copy of this volume with me.

32 Mary Shelley, Author's Introduction to the 1831 edition of *Frankenstein*, p. 57.

33 Sunstein, *Mary Shelley*, p. 119.

34 See Emma Carroll's 2016 children's novel *Strange Star* (London: Faber and Faber, 2016), which imagines a ghostly girl living at the Maison Chapuis where Mary Godwin, Percy Shelley and Claire Clairmont stayed on Lake Geneva. For literary mysteries, see Lynn Shepherd's *A Treacherous Likeness* (London: Corsair, 2013). For films, see the exuberant *Gothic*, dir. Ken Russell (1986) and *Rowing with the Wind*, dir. Gonzalo Suarez (1988). The most recent documentary concerning the Summer of 1816 is *Frankenstein and The Vampyre: A Dark and Stormy Night*, which first appeared on the BBC in 2014, produced by Oxford Films as part of the BBC's The 'Wonder of Gothic' season.

35 Jerrold E. Hogle, 'Gothic and Second-Generation Romanticism', in Angela Wright and Dale Townshend (eds), *Romantic Gothic: An Edinburgh Companion* (Edinburgh: Edinburgh University Press, 2015), pp. 112–28; p. 114.

36 George Levine and U. C. Knoepflmacher, *The Endurance of Frankenstein: Essays on Mary Shelley's Novel* (Berkeley: University of California Press, 1979).

Chapter 1

1 Richard Holmes, *The Age of Wonder: How the Romantic Generation Discovered the Beauty and Terror of Science* (London: HarperCollins), 2008.

2 Mary Shelley, *Frankenstein, or the Modern Prometheus* (1818), ed. Marilyn Butler (Oxford: Oxford University Press, 1998), p. 39.

[3] To Leigh Hunt, Putney,. *c.* 15 November 1844, quoted in *Selected Letters of Mary Wollstonecraft Shelley,* p. 333.

[4] Angela Leighton, *Shelley and the Sublime* (Cambridge: Cambridge University Press, 1984), p. 13.

[5] Mary Shelley, *Frankenstein* (1818 edn), p. 56.

[6] Mary Shelley, *Frankenstein* (1818 edn), p. 56.

[7] Mary Shelley, *Frankenstein* (1818 edn), p. 57.

[8] Fred Botting, *Gothic*, 2nd edn (London and New York: Routledge, 2014), p. 95.

[9] For a fuller account of this work, and of Mary's remoulding of the materials into the work of 1817, see Jeanne Moskal's excellent Introduction to *The Novels and Selected Works of Mary Shelley*, vol. 8: *Travel Writing*, ed. Jeanne Moskal (London: William Pickering, 1996), pp.1–4.

[10] See Charles E. Robinson, *The Frankenstein Notebooks: A Facsimile Edition of Mary Shelley's Manuscript Novel, 1816–17 (with alterations in the hand of Percy Bysshe Shelley)*, 2 vols (New York: Garland, 1996) for a full analysis of Percy Bysshe Shelley's editorial interventions in the history of *Frankenstein*. As I have already noted, Mary Shelley also took much of the descriptive force of Mont Blanc from the *History of a Six Weeks' Tour*, published in 1817, where the extensive notes on their travels were recorded. The precise descriptions of Mont Blanc in *Frankenstein* also owe more than something to Shelley's earlier Gothic work *Zastrozzi* which goes into similarly detailed descriptions of the mountains as it charts the trammelled subjectivity of its anti-heroine Matilda. When Sir Walter Scott mistakenly ascribed *Frankenstein* to Percy Shelley in his review for *Blackwood's,* the magazine corrected the error in the next edition, and reprinted part of Shelley's 'Mont Blanc', calling it 'a little poem by the husband'.

[11] Mary Shelley, *Frankenstein* (1818 edn), p. 76.

[12] See Charles Robinson on the original, now lost, version of the story which Shelley wrote in response to the ghost story writing competition in the *Frankenstein Notebooks*, vol. I, pp. lx–lxii, and Sunstein, *Mary Shelley*, p. 122.

[13] See Sunstein, *Mary Shelley*, p. 122.

[14] Mary Shelley, Preface to the 1831 edition of *Frankenstein*, p.59.

[15] Andrew Smith, 'Scientific Contexts', in Andrew Smith (ed.), *The Cambridge Companion to Frankenstein* (Cambridge: Cambridge University Press, 2016), p. 77.

16 Robert Blair, *The Grave: A Poem* (London: M. Cooper, 1743). Although this poem was composed in the middle of the eighteenth century, it is worth noting that it was anthologised throughout the Romantic period, with the Romantic poet William Blake being commissioned to provide engravings for an edition of the poem to be published by Robert Cromek in 1805. Cromek eventually rejected Blake's engravings in favour of another artist, but still put Blake's seal of approval at the beginning of the edition.

17 On Mary Wollstonecraft's infatuation with Henry Fuseli, see Sunstein, *Mary* Shelley, pp.13–14. Sunstein further records the dinner parties that both the young Mary Godwin and the 'Henry Fuselis' attended on p. 58.

18 Mary Shelley, *Frankenstein* (1818) ed. Butler, pp. 38–9.

19 Mary Shelley to Leigh Hunt, 11 September 1823, in *The Letters of Mary Wollstonecraft Shelley*, vol. 1, pp. 377–83; p. 378. Peake's play rescued *Frankenstein* from obscurity after it failed to exhaust its first print run of 500 copies. Mary Shelley reflects on the play rescuing her from obscurity in this letter, noting to Hunt, 'But lo and behold! I found myself famous! – Frankenstein had prodigious success as a drama & was about to be repeated for the 23rd night at the English opera house', *The Letters of Mary Wollstonecraft Shelley*, vol. 1, pp. 377–83; p. 378.

20 Anne K. Mellor, *Mary Shelley: Her Life, Her Fiction, Her Monsters* (London and New York: Routledge, 1988), pp. 40–1; Evelyn Fox Keller, *Secrets of Life, Secrets of Death: Essays on Language, Gender and Science* (London: Routledge, 1992), p. 49. Mellor links the genesis of the creature to Shelley's first baby girl, who had died eighteen months prior to the genesis of the novel. Her death had produced 'a recurrent dream: "Dream that my little baby came to life again; that it had only been cold, and that we rubbed it before the fire, and it lived. Awake and find no baby." Once again she was dreaming of reanimating a corpse by warming it with a "spark of life"' (Mellor, *Mary* Shelley, p. 40). For further readings of the procreative function of the novel, see also Ellen Moers's foundational account of female Gothic in *Literary Women* (Garden City, NY: Doubleday, 1976), chapters 5 and 7.

21 Mary Shelley, *Frankenstein* (1818 edn), ed. Butler, p. 9.

22 Mary Shelley, *Frankenstein* (1818 edn), ed. Butler, p. 3.

23 Smith, 'Scientific Contexts' in *The Cambridge Companion to Frankenstein*, p. 75.

24 Mary Shelley, *Frankenstein* (1818 edn), p. 33.

25 Sunstein, *Mary Shelley*, p. 112.

26 Sunstein, *Mary Shelley*, p. 113.

27 For further discussion of this, see, for example Jon Turney, *Frankenstein's Footsteps: Science, Genetics and Popular Culture*. (New Haven: Yale University Press, 1998), where the author examines how *Frankenstein* continues to influence popular ideas about biomedical sciences.

28 Christa Knellwolf and Jane Goodall, Introduction to *Frankenstein's Science: Experimentation and Discovery in Romantic Culture, 1780–1830* (Aldershot: Ashgate, 2008), p. 8.

29 William Wordsworth, *The Excursion* (1814), in *The Complete Poetical Works*, ed. John Morley. (London: MacMillan, 1888), book 8, ll. 151–6.

30 Anne K. Mellor, 'Frankenstein: A Feminist Critique of Science', in George Levine (ed.), *One Culture: Essays in Science and Literature* (Madison: University of Wisconsin Press, 1987), pp. 287–312.

31 Mary Shelley, *Frankenstein* (1818 edn), p. 36.

32 Smith, 'Scientific Contexts', p. 70.

33 Mary Shelley, *Frankenstein* (1818 edn), p. 23.

34 Mary Shelley, *Frankenstein* (1818 edn), p. 29.

35 Mary Shelley, *Frankenstein* (1818 edn), p. 23.

36 Mary Shelley, *Frankenstein* (1818 edn), p. 23.

37 Mary Shelley, *Frankenstein* (1818 edn), p. 29.

38 Mary Shelley, *Frankenstein* (1818 edn), p.79.

39 Mary Shelley, *Frankenstein* (1818 edition), ed. Butler, pp. 23, 24.

40 Mary Shelley, *Frankenstein* (1818 edn), ed. Butler, p. 24.

41 As Andrew Smith observes, however, the claim that 'electricity was a fluid would prove scientifically contentious' (Smith, 'Scientific Contexts', p. 71).

42 Mary Shelley, *Frankenstein* (1818 edn), ed. Butler, p. 25.

43 Mary Shelley, *Frankenstein* (1818 edn), ed. Butler, p. 39.

44 Wordsworth, *The Excursion*, book 8, ll.199–207.

45 Mary Shelley, 'Preface' to *Frankenstein* (1831 edn), ed. Maurice Hindle (Harmondsowrth: Penguin, 1985), p. 58.

46 Hindle, 'Introduction', in Mary Shelley, *Frankenstein*, p. 24.

47 Holmes, *The Age of Wonder*, p. 325.

48 Mary Shelley's journal entry for Monday 28 October 1816, for example, notes: 'a drawing lesson – Read the Introduction to Sir H. Davy's Chemistry – write. In the evening reads Anson's voyage and Curt.

Shelley reads Don Q. aloud after tea – Finish Anson's voyage before midnight', in *The Journals*, vol. I, p. 142.

49 Humphry Davy, *A Discourse, Introductory to a Course of Lectures on Chemistry* (1802), p. 17, quoted in *Frankenstein* (1831 edn), ed. and introd. M aurice Hindle (Harmondsworth: Penguin, 1985), p. 25.

50 See also Sharon Ruston, *Creating Romanticism: Case Studies in the Literature, Science and Medicine of the 1790s* (Basingstoke: Palgrave, 2013), and in particular chapter 4, which carries an excellent analysis of Humphry Davy's poetry, experimentation and engagement with the Sublime.

51 John [Giovanni] Aldini, *An Account of the Late Improvements in Galvanism, with a series of curious and interesting experiments performed before the commissioners of the French National Institute, and repeated lately in the anatomical theatres of London* (London: Cuthell and Martin, and Murray, 1803).

52 In a blog entry for the British Library on the science behind *Frankenstein*, Sharon Ruston also notes the biographical dimension to the Shelleys' interest in this science. Although her note relates to the death or their son William, which occurred after the publication of *Frankenstein* in 1818, it is nonetheless worth considering as an ongoing interest that Mary and Percy both shared. In Mary and Percy Shelleys' tragic personal lives, there is much evidence that they believed the dead could be successfully reanimated. For example, Percy Shelley writes of their child William Shelley's last illness: 'By the skill of the physician he was once reanimated after the process of death had actually commenced, and he lived four days after that time.' Death, it seems, could be reversed; Ruston, 'The Science of Life and Death in Mary Shelley's *Frankenstein*', *http://www.bl.uk/romantics-and-victorians/articles/the-science-of-life-and-death-in-mary-shelleys-frankenstein#sthash.DC7vSFUy.dpuf.*

53 Holmes, *The Age of Wonder*, p. 308. For further reading on the vitality debate, see chapters 6 and 7 of Holmes (pp. 235–336); Smith's 'Scientific Contexts' chapter in his *Cambridge Companion to Frankenstein*; Sharon Ruston, *Shelley and Vitality* (Basingstoke: Palgrave, 2005); and Marilyn Butler, 'The First *Frankenstein* and Radical Science', *Times Literary Supplement*, 9 (April 1993), 12–14.

54 Holmes, *The Age of Wonder*, p. 296.

55 Anon. 'An Enquiry into the Probability and Rationality of Mr. Hunter's Theory of Life, being the Subject of the first two Anatomical Lectures

delivered before the Royal College of Surgeons of London', *Quarterly Review*, 22/43 (July 1819), 1–34; 14.

56 John Milton, *Paradise Lost* (1667), ed. John Leonard (London: Penguin, 2000), book X, ll. 743–5.

57 Lisa Vargo, 'Contextualizing Sources' in Andrew Smith (ed.), *The Cambridge Companion to Frankenstein* (Cambridge: Cambridge University Press, 2016), p. 37.

58 Mary Shelley, *Frankenstein*, p. 103.

59 Mary Shelley, *Frankenstein* (1818 edn), ed. Butler, pp. 104–5.

60 Mary Shelley, *Frankenstein* (1818 edn), ed. Butler, p. 77.

61 Mary Shelley, *Frankenstein* (1818 edn), ed. Butler, p. 106.

62 Mary Shelley, *Frankenstein* (1818 edn), ed. Butler, p. 103.

63 Graham Allen, *Shelley's Frankenstein* (London: Continuum, 2008), p. 56.

64 Mary Shelley, *Frankenstein*, p. 6.

65 Mary Shelley, *Frankenstein*, p. 21.

66 Sunstein, *Mary Shelley*, p. 113.

67 U. C Knoepflmacher, 'Thoughts on the Aggression of Daughters', in George Levine and U. C. Knoepflmacher (eds), *The Endurance of Frankenstein: Essays on Mary Shelley's Novel* (Berkeley, Los Angeles: University of California Press, 1979), p. 91.

68 Percy Shelley, Preface to the 1818 edition of *Frankenstein* by Mary Shelley, ed. Marilyn Butler, p. 3. As Marilyn Butler notes, 'The unsigned Preface was written by Percy Shelley, as though author of the novel. See Mary Shelley, Introduction to 3rd edition, Appendix A: 'As far as I can recollect, it was entirely written by him' (p. 252). The allusion to the 'enervating effects of the novels of the present day' brings to mind William Wordsworth's earlier implicit denigration of the Gothic in the Preface to *Lyrical Ballads* (1800) where he complained of the 'frantic novels, sickly and stupid German tragedies and deluges of idle and extravagant stories in verse' that he perceived to be contaminating literary taste in Britain.

69 Mary Shelley, *Frankenstein* (ed. Butler), p. 3.

70 John Milton, *Areopagitica; A speech of Mr. John Milton for the Liberty of Unlicenc'd Printing, to the Parlament of England* (London: 1644).

71 Sir Walter Scott, review of *Frankenstein, or the Modern Prometheus* for *Blackwood's Edinburgh Magazine*, 2 (20 March/1 April 1818), 613–20; 613.

72 The rhetoric that Scott uses here brings to mind Joanna Baillie's 'Introductory Discourse' to her *Plays on the Passions* (1800) where she talks about anatomising the feelings and reactions of her characters. E. J. Clery's excellent chapter on Mary Shelley in *Women's Gothic* explores in detail the interconnections between Baillie's dramatic strategy and Mary Shelley's novelistic strategy. Here it is interesting to see how Sir Walter Scott also draws attention to the effect of marvellous incidents upon 'mortals like ourselves'. It is a Romantic rhetoric of commonality that was shared by Joanna Baillie, William Wordsworth in his 'Preface' to *Lyrical Ballads*, and here by Scott.

73 [John Barrow], review of Lieutenant Edward Chappell (1792–1861), *Narrative of a Voyage to Hudson's Bay, in His Majesty's Ship Rosamond, Containing Some Account of the North-Eastern Coast of America, and of the Tribes Inhabiting that Remote Region* (1817), *Quarterly Review*, 18 (October 1817), 199–223; 199–200. For further context on this, see Jessica Richard, '"A Paradise of My Own Creation": *Frankenstein* and the improbable romance of polar exploration'. *Nineteenth-Century Contexts*, 25 (2003): 295–314; Adriana Craciun, '*Frankenstein's* Politics', in *The Cambridge Companion to Frankenstein*, pp. 84–97; and Craciun, *Writing Arctic Disaster: Authorship and Exploration* (Cambridge: Cambridge University Press, 2016).

74 Mary Shelley, *Frankenstein*, p. 6.

75 Mary Shelley, *Frankenstein*, p. 6.

76 Adriana Craciun, '*Frankenstein*'s Politics', p. 91.

77 Mary Shelley, *Frankenstein*, p. 10.

78 Mary Shelley, *Frankenstein*, p. 5.

79 Mary Shelley, *Frankenstein*, p. 6.

80 Mary Shelley, *Frankenstein*, p. 183.

81 See Mary Shelley's reading list for 1815 where she lists 'Clarissa Harlowe', in *The Journals of Mary Shelley*, vol. 1, p. 90.

82 Fred Botting, *Gothic*, 2nd edn (London: Routledge, 2014), p. 93.

83 For a fuller discussion of this, see my essay 'Female Gothic' in *The Cambridge Companion to Frankenstein*, ed. Andrew Smith, 101–15.

84 Mary Shelley, *Frankenstein*, p. 5.

85 Mellor, *Mary Shelley*, chapter 3: 'My Hideous Progeny', pp. 52–69.

86 Mary and Percy married in December 1816. There has been some critical discussion (most notably by Charles Robinson, see his chapter 'Frankenstein: Its Composition and Publication' in *The Cambridge*

Companion to Frankenstein), which has argued that, as the frame narrative relating to Walton may have been added somewhere between late 1816 and early 1817, it is possible that the initials could refer to Mary Wollstonecraft Shelley.

87 Mary Wollstonecraft, *A Vindication of the Rights of Woman* (1792; Harmondsworth: Penguin, 1986), p. 266.

88 Mellor, *Mary Shelley*, p. 118.

89 In 'Vital Artifice: Mary, Percy and the Psychopolitical Intergrity of *Frankenstein*', Peter Dale Scott also notes that 'In Safie, *Frankenstein* proffers an androgynously balanced corrective to Rousseau's docile, domestic, and affectionate Sophie, a figure reproved by Mary Wollstonecraft'; in Levine and Knoepflmacher (eds), *The Endurance of Frankenstein*, pp. 172–202; p. 174.

90 Mary Shelley, *Frankenstein*, p. 99.

91 Mary Shelley, *Frankenstein*, p. 178.

92 Mary Shelley, Frankenstein, p. 179.

93 Mary Shelley, *Frankenstein*, p. 165.

94 For further readings of this, see also Beth Newman, 'Narratives of Seduction and the Seductions of Narrative: The Frame Structure of *Frankenstein*, *ELH*, 53 (1986), 141–61.

95 Mary Shelley, *Frankenstein*, p. 178.

96 Fred Botting, *Making Monstrous: Frankenstein, Criticism, Theory* (Manchester: Manchester University Press, 1991), p. 4.

97 Sir Walter Scott, review of *Frankenstein, or the Modern Prometheus* for *Blackwood's Edinburgh Magazine*, 2 (20 March/1 April 1818), 613–20

98 Mary Shelley to Sir Walter Scott, Bagni di Lucca, 14 June 1818, repr. In *Selected Letters of Mary Wollstonecraft Shelley*, ed. Betty T. Bennett (Baltimore and London: Johns Hopkins University Press, 1995), p. 34.

99 Daisy Hays, *Young Romantics* (London: Bloomsbury 2010), p. 88. Sadly, where the media have picked up on the issue of the authorship of one of the greatest and most enduring works of English literature, the response has been, to say the least, underwhelming. Germaine Greer, for one, only defended Mary Shelley's authorship in the *Guardian* because of the inferiority of the work. She criticised *Frankenstein* as having 'more loose ends than a grass skirt', arguing that 'Yes, Frankenstein really was written by Mary Shelley. It's obvious – because the book is so bad'; Germaine Greer, 'Yes, *Frankenstein* really was written by Mary Shelley. It's obvious – because the book is so bad.', *The Guardian*, 9 April 2007, *https://www.theguardian.com/world/2007/apr/09/gender.books.*

100 Mary Shelley, 'Giovanni Villani', *The Liberal*, 4 (1823), 281–97, repr. in Bennett and Robinson (eds), *The Mary Shelley Reader*, p. 330.

101 Shelley, 'Giovanni Villani', p. 330.

Chapter 2

1 Sunstein, *Mary Shelley*, p. 150.

2 Mary Shelley, *Journals*, I, p.294.

3 Frederick L. Jones (ed.), *Maria Gisborne and Edward E. Williams, Shelley's Friends: Their Journals and Letters* (Norman: University of Oklahoma Press, 1951), p. 44.

4 Dale Townshend, *The Orders of Gothic: Foucault, Lacan and the Subject of Gothic Writing, 1764–1820* (New York: AMS Press, 2007), p. 169.

5 Mary Shelley, *Matilda*, from *Mathilda*, ed. Elizabeth Nitchie, Extra Series 3 of *Studies in Philology* (Chapel Hill: The University of North Carolina Press, 1959), repr. In Bennett and Robinson (eds), *The Mary Shelley Reader*, pp. 175–246; p. 175.

6 Mary Shelley, *Matilda*, p. 175.

7 Mary Shelley, *Matilda*, p. 177.

8 Mary Shelley, *Matilda*, p. 177.

9 Mary Shelley, *Matilda*, p. 177.

10 Mary Shelley, *Matilda*, p. 178.

11 Mary Shelley, *Matilda*, p. 179.

12 William Godwin to Amelia Anderson, 23 October 1797, in *Letters of William Godwin*, vol. I, pp. 258–9.

13 Mary Shelley, *Matilda*, p. 145.

14 Mary Shelley, *Matilda*, p. 185.

15 Mary Shelley, *Matilda*, p. 185.

16 Mary Shelley, *Matilda*, p. 189.

17 Mary Shelley, *Matilda*, p. 189.

18 Mary Shelley, *Matilda*, p. 196.

19 Mary Shelley, *Matilda*, p. 197.

20 Richard Holmes, *Coleridge: Darker Reflections* (New York: HarperCollins, 2000), pp. 335–7

21 Mary Shelley, *Matilda*, p. 199.

22 Mary Shelley, *Matilda*, p. 201.

23 In relation to this, see also Charles E. Robinson, '*Mathilda* as Dramatic

Actress', in Betty T. Bennett and Stuart Curran (eds), *Mary Shelley in Her Time* (Baltimore: Johns Hopkins University Press, 2000), pp. 76–87.

24 Mary Shelley, *Matilda*, p. 201.

25 Mary Shelley, *Matilda*, p. 202.

26 Mary Shelley, *Matilda*, p. 202.

27 Mary Shelley, *Matilda*, p. 205.

28 Mary Shelley, *Matilda*, p. 215.

29 Mary Shelley, *Matilda*, p. 224.

30 Mary Shelley, *Matilda*, p. 237.

31 Michelle Faubert, 'A Family Affair: Ennobling Suicide in Mary Shelley's Matilda', *Essays in Romanticism*, 20/7 (2013), 101–28.

32 Mary Shelley, *Matilda*, p. 246.

33 Mary Shelley, *Matilda*, p. 246.

Chapter 3

1 As Tilottama Rajan records in the notes to her edition of *Valperga*, Shelley had read Machiavelli's *History of Florence* and his *La Vita de Castruccio Castraccani de Lucca* (1520), but her wider absorption of Machiavelli's thinking from his most famous work, *The Prince* (1513), informs the Realpolitik that increasingly comes to dominate the character of Castruccio (Mary Shelley, *Valperga* (1823) (Peterborough, ON: Broadview Press), p. 443).

2 Nora Crook has speculated that it was William Godwin who then went on to supplement the Preface with a further historical record of the history of Castruccio from the pen of Moreri. Crook's argument that Godwin wrote the remainder of the short Preface concerning sources for the Life of Castruccio is based on the fact that it consists of a large quotation from Moreri, an author that Godwin had read, but whom Mary Shelley had not used elsewhere (Introduction to *The Novels and Selected Works of Mary Shelley*, vol. III, p. xiii).

3 Review of Mary Shelley, *Valperga* in *The Ladies' Monthly Museum*, 17 (April 1823), 216–18.

4 Review of Mary Shelley, *Valperga* in *The Examiner*, 788 (2 March 1823), 154.

5 Jane Austen, *Northanger Abbey* (1818), ed. Marilyn Butler (Harmondsworth: Penguin, 1995), p. 97

6 Mary Shelley, *Valperga*, ed. Rajan, p. 70.

7 Percy Bysshe Shelley, 'To [A LADY] [?Spring 1821], in *The Letters of Percy Bysshe Shelley*, ed. Frederick L. Jones (Oxford: Clarendon Press, 1964), vol. II, pp. 277–8. I am grateful to my colleague Madeleine Callaghan for talking over this letter with me.

8 Mark Salber Phillips, *Society and Sentiment: Genres of Historical Writing in Britain, 1740–1820* (Princeton: Princeton University Press, 2000), p. 171.

9 Sonia Hofkosh, 'Euthanasia's Handkerchief; or, the Object at the End of History', *European Romantic Review*, 20/5 (2009), 689–97; 689.

10 See James R. Foster, 'The Abbé Prévost and the English Novel', *PMLA*, 42 (1927), 443–64.

11 Amongst many other romances, the Abbé Prévost wrote a historical romance based on the supposition that Oliver Cromwell had fathered an illegitimate son. *Le philosophe anglais ou Histoire de Monsieur Clèveland, fils naturel de Cromwell, écrite par lui-même, et traduite de l'anglais par l'auteur des Mémoires d'un homme de qualité* (1731–9) provided the model of the historical romance for later authors such as Sophia Lee and Clara Reeve.

12 Rajan, Introduction to Mary Shelley, *Valperga* (1823), p. 9.

13 Margaret Anne Doody, 'Deserts, ruins and troubled waters: female dreams in fiction and the development of the Gothic novel', *Genre*, 10 (1977), 529–72; 560.

14 As Pamela Clemit notes in her essay 'Revisiting William Godwin', the Oxford edition of *Caleb Williams* was the first to include a copy of this manuscript essay. 'The manuscript containing this essay and another one entitled "Of Scepticism" was annotated by Godwin, "These Essays were written while the Enquirer was in the press, under the impression that the favour of the public might have demanded another volume" (Bod. MS Abinger c. 86, fol. 23r), but was not published during his lifetime' ('Revisiting William Godwin' in *Oxford Handbooks Online*, December 2015, *DOI:10.1093/oxfordhb/9780199935338.013.47*. Tilottama Rajan's Broadview Press edition of *Valperga* also includes the essay in an Appendix, and it is from this source that I quote.

15 William Godwin, 'Of History and Romance' (1797), Appendix A, in Rajan (ed.), Mary Shelley, *Valperga*, pp. 469–74; 470–1, 473–4.

16 Godwin, 'Of History and Romance', p. 473.

17 Clara Reeve, *The Progress of Romance*, vol. I (London, 1785), p. 6.

18 Niccolò Machiavelli, *The Life of Castruccio Castracani of Lucca. The Works of the Famous Nicholas Machiavel, Citizen and Secretary of Florence* (London: Clavel, Harper etc., 1694), pp. 239–52; *Valperga*, ed. Rajan, pp. 475, 477.

19 Mary Shelley's reading list for 1818, it is interesting to note, included Sterne's *The Life and Opinions of Tristram Shandy, Gentleman* (1759) and *A Sentimental Journey through France and Italy, by Mr Yorick* (1768). See *The Journals of Mary Shelley, 1814-1844*, vol. I, p. 102.

20 Shelley, *Valperga*, ed. Rajan, p. 66.

21 It provides a section of Villani's account of the episode of one of several collapses of the Carraia Bridge during the May Day celebrations of 1304: 'In preparation for the May Day celebrations those of the suburb of San Friano were accustomed to make merry [in competition with other groups] in a more original and different way. They dispatched a proclamation that whoever wanted to have news from the other world should be on the bridge of Carraia and around there along the banks of the Arno on the May Day festival. They set up a stage on barges and boats in the river, and on this they represented the resemblance and the appearance of hell with flames and other suffering and torment, with men disguised as demons, terrible to behold. Others, who figured as the naked souls of people, were put through those various torments with horrible howls and screams and tempest which seemed loathsome and frightful to hear and to see. Because of the novelty of the show many citizens had to come to look. The Carraia bridge, which at the time was built on wooden pilings, was so overloaded with people that it collapsed in several places and fell with the people on it so that many died and drowned, and were hurt', from Giovanni Villani, *Villani's Chronicle: Being Selections from the First Nine Books of the Chroniche Fiorentine of Giovanni Villani*, V, ll. 17–21, pp. 360–1, in Teresa G. Frisch, *Gothic Art, 1140–c. 1450* (Toronto: University of Toronto Press, repr. 1994).

22 Mary Shelley, *Valperga*, ed. Rajan, pp. 66–7.

23 A. L. and John Aikin, 'On the Pleasure Derived from Objects of Terror', in *Miscellaneous Pieces in Prose* (London: Joseph Johnson, 1773).

24 Charles Robert Maturin, *Melmoth the Wanderer* (1820), ed. Douglas Grant, introd. Chris Baldick (Oxford: Oxford University Press, 1989), p. 257.

25 Clery, *Women's Gothic*, p. 121.

26 Mary Shelley, *Valperga*, ed. Rajan, p. 81.

27 Joseph W. Lew, 'God's Sister: History and Ideology in *Valperga*', in Audrey A. Fisch, Anne K. Mellor and Esther H. Schor (eds), *The Other Mary Shelley: Beyond Frankenstein* (Oxford and New York: Oxford University Press, 1993), pp. 159–81; p. 165.

28 Mary Shelley, *Valperga*, ed. Rajan, p. 116.

29 Mary Shelley, *Valperga*, ed. Rajan, p. 131.

30 John Milton, *Paradise Lost* (1667), ed. John Lennard, book I, ll. 588–606, p. 18.

31 Mary Shelley, *Valperga*, ed. Rajan, pp. 167–8.

32 Mary Shelley, *Valperga* (1823), ed. Rajan, pp. 199–200.

33 For a further reading of *The Monk* in relation to veiling, see my essay 'European Disruptions of the Idealized Woman', in Avril Horner (ed.), *European Gothic* (Manchester: Manchester University Press, 2002), pp. 39–54.

34 Mary Shelley, *Valperga* (1823), ed. Rajan, p. 200.

35 Barbara Jane O'Sullivan, 'Beatrice in *Valperga:* A New Cassandra', in Fisch et al. (eds), *The Other Mary Shelley*, pp. 140–58; p. 144.

36 O'Sullivan, 'Beatrice', p. 144.

37 O'Sullivan, 'Beatrice', p. 140.

38 Mary Shelley, *Valperga*, ed. Rajan, p. 214.

39 Mary Shelley, *Valperga*, ed. Rajan, p.221.

40 Mary Shelley, *Valperga*, ed. Rajan, p. 223.

41 Mary Shelley, *Valperga*, ed. Rajan, p. 227.

42 Mary Shelley, *Valperga*, ed. Rajan, p. 230.

43 Mary Shelley, *Valperga*, ed. Rajan, p. 359.

44 Mary Shelley, *Valperga*, ed. Rajan, p. 397.

45 Mary Shelley, *Valperga*, ed. Rajan, p. 396.

46 Mary Wollstonecraft, *A Vindication of the Rights of Men* (1790), in *Political Writings*, ed. Janet Todd (Oxford: Oxford University Press, 1993), p. 8.

47 David Hume, Essay 7, 'Whether the British Government Inclines M: History and Ideology in *Valperga*ore to an Absolute Monarchy, or a Republic', in *Essays, Moral and Political.* For further discussion of this, see Joseph Lew's essay 'God's Sister', in Fisch et al. (eds), *The Other Mary Shelley*, p. 162.

Chapter 4

1 Byron, as quoted in *Lady Blessington's Conversations with Lord Byron*, ed. Ernest J. Lovell, Jr (Princeton: Princeton University Press, 1969), p. 53. quoted in Sunstein, *Mary Shelley*, p. 259.

2 Sunstein, *Mary Shelley*, p. 223.

3 This letter is forthcoming in vol. XII of *Shelley and his Circle, 1773–1822*, ed. Kenneth Neill Cameron, Donald H. Reiman and Doucet Devin Fischer (Cambridge, MA: Harvard University Press, 1961–).

4 Mary Shelley, letter to Thomas Medwin, 10 May 1823, Carl and Lily Pforzheimer Collection, New York Public Library, MWS 341. This letter is all the more remarkable since relations between Mary Shelley and Thomas Medwin became so strained later, as he proceeded to publish the controversial *Conversations of Lord Byron* (1824) and the first fully published biography of Percy Bysshe Shelley in 1847.

5 Mary Shelley, 'On Ghosts', *London Magazine*, 9 (March 1824), 253–56; repr. in Bennett and Robinson (eds), *The Mary Shelley Reader*, pp. 334–40; p. 334.

6 Mary Shelley, 'On Ghosts', p. 335.

7 Mary Shelley, 'On Ghosts', pp. 335–6.

8 Mary Shelley, 'Giovanni Villani', *The Liberal*, 4 (1823), 281–97. Excerpt reprinted in Bennett and Robinson (eds), *The Mary Shelley Reader*, pp. 329–33; p. 330.

9 Mary Shelley, 'On Ghosts', p. 336.

10 In relation to this passage of 'On Ghosts', Stephen Hebron and Elizabeth Denlinger, who curated the superb exhibition 'Shelley's Ghost', reflect in the accompanying book that 'It is too much to say that Mary ever looked for, let alone saw, Shelley's ghost, but his death created a sudden void. She and her infant son were in Italy and facing an uncertain future, and images of Shelley that were almost palpable in their intensity and immediacy rushed in to fill the empty space'; *Shelley's Ghost* (Oxford: Bodleian Library, 2010), p. 98.

11 Journal entry, 24 May 1824, in *The Journals of Mary Shelley*, vol. 2, pp. 476–7.

12 Mary Shelley, Introduction to *The Last Man*, ed Anne McWhir (Peterborough, ON: Broadview Press, 1996), p. 5.

13 Mary Shelley, Introduction to *The Last Man*, p. 5.

14 Morton D. Paley in his essay '*The Last Man*: Apocalypse Without Millennium' notes that 'Since 1823 the literary world had been preoccupied with a controversy about just who had invented the Last Man, beginning with the publication of Thomas Campbell's "The Last Man" and Francis Jeffrey's suggestion in *The Edinburgh Review* that Campbell was indebted to Byron's "Darkness" for the idea. Campbell was moved to print an open letter to Jeffrey asserting his own priority and claiming that it was he who at least fifteen years before had suggested to Byron the subject', in Audrey Fisch et al. (eds), *The Other Mary Shelley*, pp. 107–23; p. 107.

15 Lord Byron, 'Darkness' (1816), in *The Prisoner of Chillon and Other Poems* (1816), ll.1–15.

16 Wood, *Tambora*, p. 95.

17 Mary Shelley, *The Last Man* (1826), ed. Anne McWhir (Peterborough, ON: Broadview Press, 1996), p. 51.

18 Mary Shelley, letter to Thomas Medwin, 10 May 1823.

19 Milton, *Paradise Lost*, book XI, ll. 770–2, p. 267.

20 Mary Shelley, *The Last Man*, p. 10.

21 Mary Shelley, *The Last Man*, pp. 21 and 14.

22 Mary Shelley, *The Last Man*, p. 17.

23 Mary Shelley, *The Last Man*, p. 14.

24 Byron, *Manfred, A Dramatic Poem* (1817), Act II, sc. ii, ll. 55–6. Composed between September 1816 and February 1817, *Manfred* is also a by-product of the intense Summer of 1816 in its tale of Faustian bargaining and tormented solitude. It was undoubtedly influenced by the Alpine setting around Lake Geneva, and also by Matthew Lewis's visit to the Villa Diodati in August 1816, where he spontaneously translated Goethe's *Faustus* for Byron and Percy Shelley. Mary Shelley may not have been present for the translation of *Faustus* as she claimed to be intimidated by the cosmopolitan company that Byron was entertaining during late August, but Shelley was.

25 Mary Shelley, *The Last Man*, p. 15.

26 Mary Shelley, *The Last Man*, p. 21.

27 Sunstein, *Mary Shelley*, p. 100.

28 Mary Shelley, *The Last Man*, p. 39.

29 Paley, *The Last Man*, p. 113.

30 Mary Shelley, *The Last Man*, p. 202.

31 Mary Shelley, *The Last Man*, p. 189.

[32] Mary Shelley, *The Last Man*, p. 201.
[33] *Journals of Mary Shelley, 1814–1844*, vol. I, p. 56.
[34] Mary Shelley, *The Last Man*, p. 199.
[35] Mary Shelley, *The Last Man*, p. 220.
[36] Mary Shelley, *The Last Man*, p. 121.
[37] Mary Shelley, *The Last Man*, p. 221.
[38] Mary Shelley, *The Last Man*, pp. 308–9.
[39] Mary Shelley, *The Last Man*, p. 312.
[40] Mary Shelley, *The Last Man*, pp. 330–1.
[41] Mary Shelley, *The Last Man*, p. 327.
[42] 'The Choice', Bodleian Library, Oxford, Abinger Deposit d.311/4, l. 118.
[43] Mary Shelley, 'To the Dead', 15 December 1834, one-page folio autograph manuscript poem from the Carl H. Pforzheimer Collection, New York Public Library.
[44] See Anne K. Mellor's chapter 'Love, Guilt and Reparation: *The Last Man*', in *Mary Shelley: Her Life, her Fiction, her Monsters* (New York and London: Routledge, 1988), p. 150.
[45] Mary Shelley, *The Last Man*, p. 327.

Chapter 5

[1] Baculard d'Arnaud, *Nouvelles Historiques*. 3 vols (Paris: Delalain, 1774–83); Sophia Lee (trans.), *Warbeck: A Pathetic Tale*, 2 vols (London: William Lane, 1786). For a further discussion of d'Arnaud and Lee's versions of *Warbeck*, see chapter 2, 'The Translator Cloak'd', in my *Britain, France and the Gothic*, pp. 50–1. For more detailed readings of Mary Shelley's *The Fortunes of Perkin Warbeck* (1830), see Lidia Garbin, 'Mary Shelley and Walter Scott: *The Fortunes of Perkin Warbeck* and the Historical Novel', in Michael Eberle-Sinatra (ed.), *Mary Shelley's Fictions: From Frankenstein to Falkner* (Basingstoke: Palgrave, 2000), pp. 150–63; and William D. Brewer, 'William Godwin, Chivalry, and Mary Shelley's *The Fortunes of Perkin Warbeck*', *Papers on Language and Literature*, 35/2 (Spring 1999), 187–205.
[2] See, for example, Nora Crook, 'In Defence of the 1831 *Frankenstein*' in Eberle-Sinatra (ed.), *Mary Shelley's Fictions*, pp. 3–21.
[3] Ann Radcliffe, 'On the Supernatural in Poetry', *The New Monthly Magazine and Literary Journal*, 16/1 (1826), 145 –52; 149.

4 Radcliffe, 'On the Supernatural in Poetry', 147–8.
5 Mary Shelley, Introduction to *Frankenstein* for *the* Standard Novels Edition issued by Colburn and Bentley (1831), pp. 56–7.
6 Mary Shelley, Author's Introduction, in *Frankenstein* (1831), pp. 56–7.
7 Mary Shelley, Author's Introduction, in *Frankenstein* (1831), p. 59.
8 Eleanor Sleath, *The Orphan of the Rhine* (London: William Lane, 1798).
9 Mary Shelley, *Frankenstein* (1831), p. 83.
10 Mary Shelley, *Frankenstein* (1831), p. 84.
11 Mary Shelley, *Frankenstein* (1831), p. 85.
12 George Eliot, *Middlemarch*, chapter 27.
13 Mary Shelley, 'Transformation' (1831) first published in *The Keepsake for MDCCCXXXI,* ed. Frederic Mansel Reynolds (London: Hurst, Chance and Co, [1830], pp.18–39; repr. in Bennett and Robinson, *The Mary Shelley Reader*, pp. 286–300; p. 289.
14 Mary Shelley, 'Transformation', p. 289.
15 Mary Shelley, 'Transformation', p. 291.
16 Mary Shelley, 'Transformation', p. 292.
17 Mary Shelley, 'Transformation', p. 300.
18 Mary Shelley, 'Transformation', p. 300.
19 Mary Shelley, 'Transformation', p. 300.
20 Mary Shelley, 'The Mortal Immortal: A Tale', in Frederic Mansel Edwards (ed.), *The Keepsake* for 1833 (London: Longman, Rees, Orme, Brown, Green and Longman), pp. 71–87; repr. in Bennett and Robinson, *The Mary Shelley Reader*, pp. 314–26; p. 314.
21 Mary Shelley, 'The Mortal Immortal', p. 314.
22 Mary Shelley, 'The Mortal Immortal', p. 317.

Conclusion

1 Mary Shelley, *Frankenstein* (1818), ed. Marilyn Butler, p. 17.
2 See note 2 in Bennett and Robinson's edition of the tale in *The Mary Shelley Reader*, pp. 263–73; p. 263.
3 Sunstein, *Mary* Shelley, p. 193.
4 Mary Shelley, 'The Bride of Modern Italy' (1824), first published in the *London Magazine*, 9 (April 1824); repr. in Bennett and Robinson (eds), *The Mary Shelley Reader*, pp.263–73; p. 263.
5 Mary Shelley, 'The Bride of Modern Italy', p. 265.

[6] Mary Shelley, 'The Bride of Modern Italy', p. 266.

[7] Mary Shelley, letter to Charles Ollier, 10 February 1833, in *Selected Letters of Mary Wollstonecraft Shelley*, pp. 249–50. Mary writes to Ollier, 'Do you know when my Novel is due to go to the press – I am ready when you are' (p. 249). As Bennett's note to the letter indicates, the date of 10 February was in fact an error for what should have read 10 November 1833.

[8] See Fiona Stafford, '*"Lodore": A Tale of the Present Time?*' in Eberle-Sinatra (ed.), *Mary Shelley's Fictions*. pp. 181–93; and Julie A. Carlson, *England's First Family of Writers* (Baltimore: Johns Hopkins University Press, 2007), p. 121. Stafford lists as examples of contemporaneous silver -fork novels Edward Bulwer's *Pelham* (1828) and Catherine Gore's *Women as They Are, or the Manners of the Day, Pin Money, The Tuileries, Mothers and Daughters: A Tale of the Year 1830, The Opera, The Fair of May Fair, The Sketch Book of Fashion*, and *Polish Tales*, all produced between 1830 and 1833 (Stafford, '*Lodore*', p. 182).

[9] Mary Shelley, *Lodore* (1835), ed. Lisa Vargo (Peterborough, ON: Broadview Press, 1997), pp. 321–2.

[10] Mary Shelley, *Lodore*, p. 323.

Bibliography

I Writings by Mary Shelley

Mounseer Nongtongpaw; or, the Discoveries of John Bull in a Trip to Paris (London: Proprietors of the Juvenile Library [M. J. Godwin & Co.], 1808).

[with Percy Shelley] *History of a Six Weeks' Tour through a part of France, Switzerland, Germany and Holland: with Letters Descriptive of a Sail round the Lake of Geneva, and of the Glaciers of Chamouni* (London: T. Hookham, and C. and J. Ollier, 1817); repr. in *The Novels and Selected Works of Mary Shelley* (gen. eds Nora Crook with Pamela Clemit), vol. 8: *Travel Writing*, ed. Jeanne Moskal (London: William Pickering, 1996).

Frankenstein, or the Modern Prometheus (1818), ed. Marilyn Butler (Oxford: Oxford University Press, 1994).

Frankenstein, or the Modern Prometheus (1831), ed. Maurice Hindle (Harmondsworth: Penguin, 1985).

Frankenstein; or, The Modern Prometheus, ed. Nora Crook, introd. Betty T. Bennett, vol. 1 of *The Novels and Selected Works of Mary Shelley* (gen. eds Nora Crook with Pamela Clemit) (London: William Pickering. 1996).

Matilda (1819), first edited and published by Elizabeth Nitchie as *Mathilda* (Chapel Hill: University of North Carolina Press, 1959), in Betty T. Bennett and Charles E. Robinson (eds), *The Mary Shelley Reader* (New York and Oxford: Oxford University Press, 1990).

Valperga (1823), ed. Tilottama Rajan (Peterborough, ON: Broadview Press, 1998).

The Last Man (1826), ed. Anne McWhir (Peterborough, ON: Broadview Press, 1996).

The Fortunes of Perkin Warbeck: A Romance, ed. Doucet Devin Fischer, vol. 5 of *The Novels and Selected Works of Mary Shelley* (gen. eds Nora Crook with Pamela Clemit) (London: William Pickering, 1996).

Lodore. (1835), ed. Lisa Vargo (Peterborough, ON: Broadview Press, 1997).

Falkner: A Novel (1837), ed. Pamela Clemit, vol. 7 of *The Novels and Selected Works of Mary Shelley* (gen. eds Nora Crook with Pamela Clemit) (London: William Pickering, 1996).

The Letters of Mary Wollstonecraft Shelley, ed. Betty T. Bennett, 2 vols (Baltimore and London: The Johns Hopkins University Press, 1980).

Selected Letters of Mary Wollstonecraft Shelley, ed. Betty T. Bennett (Baltimore and London: The Johns Hopkins University Press, 1995).

The Journals of Mary Shelley, 1814–1844, ed. Paula R. Feldman and Diana Scott-Kilvert (Oxford: Clarendon Press, 1987).

Letter to Thomas Medwin, 10 May 1823, Carl H. Pforzheimer Collection, New York Public Library, MWS 341.

'Giovanni Villani', *The Liberal*, 4 (1823), 281–97; repr. in *The Mary Shelley Reader*, ed. Betty T. Bennett and Charles E. Robinson (Oxford: Oxford University Press, 2000), pp. 330–3.

'On Ghosts', *London Magazine*, 9 (March 1824), 253–6; repr, in *The Mary Shelley Reader*, ed. Betty T. Bennett and Charles E. Robinson (New York and Oxford: Oxford University Press, 1990), pp. 334–40.

'The Mortal Immortal: A Tale' in *The Keepsake* for 1833, ed. Frederic Mansel Reynolds (London: Longman, Rees, Orme, Brown, Green and Longman, 1832), pp.71–87; repr. in *The Mary Shelley Reader*, ed. Betty T. Bennett and Charles E. Robinson (New York and Oxford: Oxford University Press, 1990), pp. 314–26.

'Transformation' in *The Keepsake* for 1831, ed. Frederic Mansel Reynolds (London: Hurst, Chance and Co. [1830]); repr. in *The Mary Shelley Reader*, ed. Betty T. Bennett and Charles E. Robinson (New York and Oxford: Oxford University Press, 1990), pp. 286–300.

'The Choice', Abinger Deposit, Bodleian Library, Oxford, 311/4.

'To the Dead', 15 December 1834. one-page folio autograph manuscript poem from the Carl H. Pforzheimer Collection, New York Public Library.

II Biographies of Mary Shelley and Her Circle

Hay, Daisy, *Young Romantics: The Shelleys, Byron and Other Tangled Lives* (London: Bloomsbury, 2010).

Hebron, Stephen and Elizabeth Denlinger, *Shelley's Ghost: Reshaping the Image of a Literary Family* (Oxford: Bodleian Library, 2010).

Holmes, Richard, *The Age of Wonder: How the Romantic Generation Discovered the Beauty and Terror of Science* (London: HarperCollins, 2008).

Jones, Frederick L., *Maria Gisborne and Edward E. Williams, Shelley's Friends: Their Journals and Letters* (Norman: University of Oklahoma Press, 1951).

Seymour, Miranda, *Mary Shelley* (London: Faber and Faber, 2000).

St Clair, William, *The Godwins and the Shelleys: The Biography of a Family* (London: Faber and Faber, 1989).

Sunstein, Emily W., *Mary Shelley: Romance and Reality* (Baltimore: The Johns Hopkins University Press, 1989.

III Critical Studies of Mary Shelley's Writing

Allen, Graham, *Shelley's Frankenstein* (London: Continuum, 2008).

Anon., review of Mary Shelley, *Valperga*, *The Ladies' Monthly Museum*, 17 (April 1823), 216–18.

Anon., review of Mary Shelley, *Valperga*, *The Examiner*, 788 (2 March 1823), 154.

Baldick, Chris, *In Frankenstein's Shadow: Myth, Monstrosity, and Nineteenth-century Writing* (Oxford: Clarendon Press, 1987).

Bennett, Betty, and Stuart Curran, *Mary Shelley in Her Times* (Baltimore: Johns Hopkins University Press, 2000).

Botting, Fred, *Making Monstrous: Frankenstein, Criticism, Theory* (Manchester: Manchester University Press, 1991).

Brewer, William D., 'William Godwin, Chivalry, and Mary Shelley's *The Fortunes of Perkin Warbeck*', *Papers on Language and Literature*, 35/2 (Spring 1999), 187–205.

Butler, Marilyn, 'The First *Frankenstein* and Radical Science', *Times Literary Supplement* (9 April 1993), 12–14.

Carlson, Julie A., *England's First Family of Writers: Mary Wollstonecraft, William Godwin, Mary Shelley* (Baltimore: Johns Hopkins University Press, 2007).

Clery, E. J., *Women's Gothic: From Clara Reeve to Mary Shelley* (Tavistock: Northcote House, 2000).

Craciun, Adriana, '*Frankenstein*'s politics', in Andrew Smith (ed.), *The Cambridge Companion to Frankenstein* (Cambridge: Cambridge University Press, 2016), pp. 84 –97.

—— *Writing Arctic Disaster: Authorship and Exploration* (Cambridge: Cambridge University Press, 2016).

Crook, Nora, 'Mary Shelley, Author of *Frankenstein*', in David Punter (ed.), *A Companion to the Gothic* (Oxford: Blackwell 2000), pp. 58–69.

—— 'In Defence of the 1831 *Frankenstein*', in Michael Eberle-Sinatra (ed.), *Mary Shelley's Fictions: From Frankenstein to Falkner* (Basingstoke: Palgrave, 2000), 3–21.

Faubert, Michelle, 'A Family Affair: Ennobling Suicide in Mary Shelley's *Matilda*', *Essays in Romanticism*, 20/7 (2013), 101–28.

Fisch, Audrey A., Anne K. Mellor and Esther H. Schor, *The Other Mary Shelley: Beyond Frankenstein* (New York and Oxford: Oxford University Press, 1993).

Garbin, Lidia, 'Mary Shelley and Walter Scott: *The Fortunes of Perkin Warbeck* and the Historical Novel', in Michael Eberle-Sinatra (ed.), *Mary Shelley's Fictions: From Frankenstein to Falkner* (Basingstoke: Palgrave, 2000), 150–63.

Hofkosh, Sonia, 'Euthanasia's Handkerchief; or, the Object at the End of History', *European Romantic Review*, 20/5 (2009), 689–97.

Hogle, Jerrold E., '*Frankenstein* as neo-gothic: from the ghost of the counterfeit to the monster of abjction', in *Romanticism, History and the Possibilities of Genre*, eds. Tilottama Rajan and Julian Wright (Cambridge: Cambridge University Press, 1998), 176–212.

Knellwolf, Christa and Jane Goodall (eds), *Frankenstein's Science: Experimentation and Discovery in Romantic Culture, 1780–1830* (Aldershot: Ashgate, 2008).

Levine, George and U. C. Knoepflmacher (eds), *The Endurance of Frankenstein* (Berkeley, Los Angeles and London: University of California Press, 1979).

Lew, Joseph W., 'God's Sister: History and Ideology in *Valperga*', in Audrey A. Fisch, Anne K. Mellor and Esther H. Schor (eds), *The Other Mary Shelley: Beyond Frankenstein* (Oxford and New York: Oxford University Press, 1993), pp. 159–81.

Mellor, Anne K., 'Frankenstein: A Feminist Critique of Science', in George Levine (ed.), *One Culture: Essays in Science and Literature* (Madison: University of Wisconsin Press, 1987), pp. 287–312.

—— *Mary Shelley: Her Life, Her Fiction, Her Monsters* (London and New York: Routledge, 1988).

Moers, Ellen, *Literary Women* (Garden City, NY: Doubleday, 1976).

Newman, Beth, 'Narratives of Seduction and the Seductions of Narrative: The Frame Structure of *Frankenstein*'. *ELH*, 53 (1986), 141–61.

O'Sullivan, Barbara Jane, 'Beatrice in *Valperga*: A New Cassandra', in Audrey A. Fisch, Anne K. Mellor and Esther H. Schor, *The Other Mary Shelley: Beyond Frankenstein* (Oxford and New York: Oxford University Press, 1993).

Paley, Morton D., '*The Last Man:* Apocalypse Without Millennium', in Audrey Fisch, Anne K. Mellor and Esther Schor (eds), *The Other Mary Shelley: Beyond Frankenstein* (New York and Oxford: Oxford University Press, 1993), 107–23.

Poovey, Mary, *The Proper Lady and the Woman Writer: Ideology as Style in the Works of Mary Wollstonecraft, Mary Shelley, and Jane Austen* (Chicago: University of Chicago Press, 1984).

Richard, Jessica, '"A Paradise of My Own Creation": *Frankenstein* and the improbable romance of polar exploration', *Nineteenth-Century Contexts,* 25 (2003), 295–314.

Robinson, Charles E., *The Frankenstein Notebooks: A Facsimile Edition of Mary Shelley's Manuscript Novel, 1816–17 (with alterations in the hand of Percy Bysshe Shelley)*, 2 vols (New York: Garland, 1996).

—— Robinson, Charles E., '*Mathilda* as Dramatic Actress', in Betty T. Bennett and Stuart Curran (eds), *Mary Shelley in Her Times* (Baltimore: Johns Hopkins University Press, 2000), pp. 76–87.

Ruston, Sharon, 'The Science of Life and Death in Mary Shelley's *Frankenstein*', British Library: *http://www.bl.uk/romantics-and-victorians/articles/the-science-of-life-and-death-in-mary-shelleys-frankenstein#sthash.DC7vSFUy.dpuf.*

Schor, Esther (ed.), *The Cambridge Companion to Mary Shelley* (Cambridge: Cambridge University Press, 2003).

Sherwin, Paul, '*Frankenstein*: Creation as Catastrophe', *PMLA*, 96/5 (1981), 883–903.

Smith, Andrew (ed.), *The Cambridge Companion to Frankenstein* (Cambridge: Cambridge University Press, 2016).

—— 'Scientific Contexts', in Andrew Smith (ed.), *The Cambridge Companion to Frankenstein* (Cambridge: Cambridge University Press, 2016), 69–83.

Stafford, Fiona, '"*Lodore*": A Tale of the Present Time?', in Michael

Eberle-Sinatra (ed.), *Mary Shelley's Fictions: From Frankenstein to Falkner* (Basingstoke: Palgrave, 2000), pp. 181–93.

Vargo, Lisa, 'Contextualizing Sources', in Andrew Smith (ed.), *The Cambridge Companion to Frankenstein* (Cambridge: Cambridge University Press, 2016), 26–40.

Veeder, William, *Mary Shelley and Frankenstein: The Fate of Androgyny* (Chicago: University of Chicago Press, 1986).

Wright, Angela, 'Female Gothic', in Andrew Smith (ed.), *The Cambridge Companion to Frankenstein* (Cambridge: Cambridge University Press, 2016), 101–115.

IV Other primary sources consulted

Aikin, A. L. and John, 'On the Pleasure Derived from Objects of Terror', in *Miscellaneous Pieces in Prose* (London: Joseph Johnson, 1773).

Aldini, [Giovanni] John, *An Account of the Late Improvements in Galvanism, with a series of curious and interesting experiments performed before the commissioners of the French National Institute, and repeated lately in the anatomical theatres of London* (London: Cuthell and Martin, and Murray, 1803).

Anon., 'An Enquiry into the Probability and Rationality of Mr. Hunter's Theory of Life, being the Subject of the first two Anatomical Lectures delivered before the Royal College of Surgeons of London', *Quarterly Review*, 22/43 (July 1819), 1–34.

d'Arnaud, Baculard, *Nouvelles Historiques*, 3 vols (Paris: Delalain, 1774–83).

Austen, Jane, *Northanger Abbey* (1818), ed. Marilyn Butler (Harmondsworth: Penguin, 1995).

Baillie, Joanna, Introductory Discourse, *A Series of plays: In which it is attempted to delineate the stronger passions of the mind. Each passion being the subject of a tragedy and a comedy* (London: Cadell, Jr and Davies, 1798), pp. 1–72.

[Barrow, John], review of Lieutenant Edward Chappell (1792–1861), 'Narrative of a Voyage to Hudson's Bay, in His Majesty's Ship Rosamond, Containing Some Account of the North-Eastern Coast of America, and of the Tribes Inhabiting that Remote Region', *Quarterly Review*, 18 (October 1817), 199–223.

Blair, Robert, *The Grave: A Poem* (London: M. Cooper, 1743).

Burke, Edmund, *A Philosophical Enquiry into the Origin of our Ideas of the Sublime and Beautiful* (1757), ed. David Womersley (London: Penguin, 1998).

Byron, George Gordon, *The Prisoner of Chillon and Other Poems* (London: John Murray,1816).

—— *Manfred, A Dramatic Poem* (London: John Murray, 1817).

Coleridge, Samuel Taylor. *Kubla Khan and Other Poems* (London: John Murray, 1816).

—— review of *The Monk, Critical Review*, 19 (February, 1797), 194–200, quoted in *Gothic Documents: A Sourcebook 1700–1820*, ed. E. J. Clery and Robert Miles (Manchester: Manchester University Press, 2000), pp. 185–9.

Davy, Humphry, *A Discourse, Introductory to a Course of Lectures on Chemistry, Delivered in the Theatre of the Royal Institution on the 21st of January, 1802* (London: Sold at the House of the Royal Institution, 1802).

Eliot, George, *Middlemarch, or a Tale of Provincial Life* (1871–2), ed. David Carroll, introd. Felicia Bonaparte (Oxford: Oxford University Press, 2008).

Eyriès, Jean-Baptiste, *Fantasmagoriana, ou receuil d'histoires d'apparitions de spectres, revenans, fantômes etc.* (Paris: F. Schoell, 1812).

[Galvani, Luigi] Aloysii Galvani, *De viribus electricitatis in motu musculari commentarius. Cum Joannis Aldini dissertatione et notis. Accesserunt epistolæ ad animalis electricitatis theoriam pertinentes* [*The Effects of Artificial Electricity on Muscular Motion*] (Mutinae [Modena] 1792).

Godwin, William, *Enquiry Concerning Political Justice, and its Influence on Political Happiness* (1793), 2nd edn (London: G. G. and J. Robinson, 1796).

—— *Things as they are; or the adventures of Caleb Williams* (1794), ed. Maurice Hindle (Harmondsworth: Penguin, 1988).

—— *Memoirs of Mary Wollstonecraft* (1798) (London: Constable, 1928).

—— *St. Leon* (1799, ed. Pamela Clemit (Oxford: Oxford University Press, 1994).

—— [Edward Baldwin], *The Pantheon, or Ancient History of the Gods of Greece and Rome* (London: 1806).

—— *The Letters of William Godwin*, ed. Pamela Clemit, 2 vols (Oxford: Oxford University Press, 2014).

Hurd, Richard, *Letters on Chivalry and Romance* (London: Millar, 1762).

Lee, Sophia, *The Recess; or, A Tale of Other* Times, 3 vols (London: Cadell, 1783; 1785 for vols. II and III).

—— (trans.), *Warbeck: A Pathetic Tale*, 2 vols (London: William Lane, 1786).

Lewis, Matthew Gregory, *The Monk; a Romance* (1796), ed. D. L. MacDonald and Kathleen Scherf (Peterboroough, ON: Broadview Press, 2004).

Lovell, Ernest J., Jr (ed.), *Lady Blessington's Conversations with Lord Byron* (Princeton: Princeton University Press, 1969).

Machiavelli, Niccolò, 'The Life of Castruccio Castracani of Lucca', in *The Works of the Famous Nicholas Machiavel, Citizen and Secretary of Florence* (London: Clavel, Harper etc., 1694), pp. 239–52.

Maturin, Charles Robert, *Melmoth the Wanderer* (1820), ed. Douglas Grant, introd. Chris Baldick (Oxford: Oxford University Press, 1989).

Milton, John, *Areopagitica; A speech* of *Mr. John Milton for the Liberty of Unlicenc'd Printing, to the Parlament of England* (London: 1644).

—— *Paradise Lost* (1667), ed. John Leonard (London: Penguin, 2000).

Peake, Richard Brinsley, *Presumption; or, The Fate of Frankenstein* (1823), in Jeffrey N. Cox (ed.), *Seven Gothic Dramas 1879–1825* (Athens: Ohio State University Press, 1992).

Polidori, John William, *The Diary of Dr. John William Polidori, 1816, Relating to Byron, Shelley, etc.*, ed. William Michael Rossetti (London: Elkin Mathews, 1911).

—— *The Vampyre* (1819) (Oxford: Woodstock Books, 1990).

Prévost d'Exiles, A.-F., *Le Philosophe anglais ou histoire de M. Clèveland (fils naturel de Cromwell), écrite par lui-même, et traduit de l'anglais par l'auteur des Mémoires d'un homme de qualité*, vol. 2, in *Oeuvres de Prévost*, 8 vols [Paris: 1731–9], ed. Jean Sgard (Grenoble: Presses Universitaires de Grenoble, 1978).

Reeve, Clara, *The Old English Baron: A Gothic Story* (1778), ed. and introd. J. Trainer (Oxford: Oxford University Press, 1967).

—— *The Progress of Romance*, 2 vols (Colchester: W. Keymer, 1785).

Richardson, Samuel, *Clarissa, or, the history of a young lady* (London: A. Millar, 1748).

Rousseau, Jean-Jacques, *La Nouvelle Héloïse* (1761); trans. William Kenrick, *Eloisa: or, a series of original letters collected and published by J. J. Rousseau*, 4 vols (London: Griffiths, Becket and De Hondt, 1761).

—— *Émile, ou de l'éducation* (1762), trans. William Kenrick, *Emilius and Sophia: or, a new system of education* (London: Griffiths, Becket and De Hondt, 1762).

Radcliffe, Ann, *A Sicilian Romance* (1790), ed. Alison Milbanke (Oxford: Oxford University Press, 1993).

—— *The Mysteries of Udolpho; a Romance* (1794), ed. Bonamy Dobrée (Oxford: Oxford University Press, 1980).

—— *The Italian, or the confessional of the black penitents* (1797), ed. Robert Miles (Harmondsworth: Penguin, 2000).

—— 'On the Supernatural in Poetry', *The New Monthly Magazine and Literary Journal*, 16/1 (1826), 145–52.

Scott, Walter, 'Remarks on *Frankenstein, or the Modern Prometheus*; a Novel', *Blackwood's Edinburgh Magazine*, 2 (20 March/1 April 1818), 613–20.

Shelley, P. B., *Zastrozzi: A Romance* (1810), in *Zastrozzi* and *St. Irvyne*, ed. Stephen C. Behrendt (Peterborough, ON: Broadview Press, 2002).

—— *Shelley and his Circle, 1773–1822*, 10 vols, ed. Kenneth Neill Cameron, Donald H. Reiman and Doucet Devin Fischer (Cambridge, MA: Harvard University Press, 1961–).

—— 'Mont Blanc' (1817), in *Shelley's Poetry and Prose*, ed. Donald H. Reiman and Neil Fraistat (New York and London: Norton, 2002).

—— *The Cenci* (1819), in *Shelley's Poetry and Prose*, ed. Donald H. Reiman and Neil Fraistat (New York and London: Norton, 2002).

—— *Prometheus Unbound* (1820), in *Shelley's Poetry and Prose*, ed. Donald H. Reiman and Neil Fraistat (New York and London: Norton, 2002).

—— 'Ode to the West Wind' (1819), in *Shelley's Poetry and Prose*, ed. Donald H. Reiman and Neil Fraistat (New York and London: Norton, 2002).

—— Letter to 'A Lady' in *The Letters of Percy Bysshe Shelley*, ed. Frederick L. Jones, 2 vols (Oxford: Clarendon Press, 1964).

Sleath, Eleanor, *The Orphan of the Rhine: A Romance*, 4 vols (London: William Lane, 1798).

Walpole, Horace, *The Castle of Otranto* (1764), ed. E. J. Clery (Oxford: Oxford University Press, 1996).

—— *The Mysterious Mother* (1768), in *The Works of Horatio Walpole, Earl of Orford*, ed. R. Walpole and M. Berry, 5 vols (London: G. G. and J. Robinson, 1798).

Wollstonecraft, Mary. (1790), *A Vindication of the Rights of Men*, in *Political Writings*, ed. Janet Todd (Oxford: Oxford University Press, 1993).

—— *Mary* and *The Wrongs of Woman* (1788/1798), ed. Gary Kelly (Oxford: Oxford University Press, 1980).

—— review of *The Italian*, *The Analytical Review: Or, History of Literature*, 25/5 (May 1797), 516–20.

Wordsworth, William. Preface to *Other Poems*, 2 vols, 2nd edn (London: Longman and Rees, 1800).

—— *The Excursion*, ed. John Morley, in *William Wordsworth: The Complete Poetical Works* (London: Macmillan, 1888).

V Other works consulted

Botting, Fred, *Gothic*, 2nd edn (London and New York: Routledge, 2014).

Clemit, Pamela, 'Revisiting William Godwin', in *Oxford Handbooks Online* (December 2015), *DOI:10.1093/oxfordhb/9780199935338.013.47*

D'Arcy Wood, Gillen, *Tambora: The Eruption that Changed the World* (Princeton: Princeton University Press, 2014).

Doody, Margaret Anne, 'Deserts, ruins and troubled waters: female dreams in fiction and the development of the Gothic novel', *Genre*, 10 (1977), 529–72.

Duffy, Cian, *Shelley and the Revolutionary Sublime* (Cambridge: Cambridge University Press, 2005).

Foster, James R., 'The Abbé Prévost and the English Novel', *PMLA*, 42 (1927), 443–64.

Frisch, Teresa G., *Gothic Art, 1140–c. 1450* (Toronto: University of Toronto Press: repr. 1994).

Gamer, Michael, 'Genres for the Prosecution: Pornography and the Gothic', *PMLA*, 114/5 (1999), 1043–54.

Hogle, Jerrold E. 'Gothic and Second-Generation Romanticism', in Angela Wright and Dale Townshend (eds), *Romantic Gothic: An Edinburgh Companion* (Edinburgh: Edinburgh University Press, 2015), pp. 112–28.

Holmes, Richard, *Coleridge: Darker Reflections* (New York: HarperCollins, 2000).

Jones, Vivien, 'The Death of Mary Wollstonecraft', *British Journal for Eighteenth-Century Studies,* 20/2 (1997), 187–205.

Keller, Evelyn Fox, *Secrets of Life, Secrets of Death: Essays on Language, Gender and Science* (London: Routledge, 1992).

Leighton, Angela, *Shelley and the Sublime* (Cambridge: Cambridge University Press, 1984).

Phillips, Mark Salber, *Society and Sentiment: Genres of Historical Writing in Britain, 1740–1820* (Princeton: Princeton University Press, 2000).

Ruston, Sharon, *Shelley and Vitality* (Basingstoke: Palgrave, 2005).

—— *Creating Romanticism: Case Studies in the Literature, Science and Medicine of the 1790s* (Basingstoke: Palgrave, 2013).

St Clair, William, *The Reading Nation in the Romantic Period* (Cambridge: Cambridge University Press, 2004).

Townshend, Dale, *The Orders of Gothic: Foucault, Lacan and the Subject of Gothic Writing, 1764–1820* (New York: AMS Press, 2007).

Townshend, Dale and Angela Wright (eds), *Ann Radcliffe, Romanticism and the Gothic* (Cambridge: Cambridge University Press, 2014).

Turney, Jon, *Frankenstein's Footsteps: Science, Genetics and Popular Culture* (New Haven: Yale University Press, 1998).

Wright, Angela, *Britain, France and the Gothic, 1764–1820: The Import of Terror* (Cambridge: Cambridge University Press, 2013).

Wright, Angela and Dale Townshend, *Romantic Gothic: An Edinburgh Companion* (Edinburgh: Edinburgh University Press, 2015).

VI Some Filmic, Musical, Documentary and Fictional Representations of the Summer of 1816

The following is by no means exhaustive, but suggests some places to begin watching or reading.

Films

Passer, Ivan (dir.), *Haunted Summer* (1988).

Russell, Ken (dir.), *Gothic* (1986).

Suarez, Gonzalo (dir.), *Rowing with the Wind* (1988).

Documentary

Smith, Philip (dir.), *Frankenstein* and *The Vampyre: A Dark and Stormy Night* (2014; first shown on BBC2).

Song

Rasputina, '1816: The Year Without a Summer', from the album *Oh Perilous World* (Rykodisc, 2007).

Novels

Carroll, Emma, *Strange Star* (London: Faber and Faber, 2016).

Shepherd, Lynn, *A Treacherous Likeness* (London: Corsair, 2013).

Index